JOHN HENRY NEWMAN

Also by Roderick Strange

The Catholic Faith
Living Catholicism
The Risk of Discipleship

Praise for *The Catholic Faith*

'[Roderick Strange] is loyal to the Church's dogmatic and moral teaching, yet the whole work is shot through with living theology. It is based both on his deep knowledge of the Catholic faith and on his own pastoral experience of people's needs, as his fund of real-life stories in the book testifies.' *The Universe*

'Here is a coherently expounded faith which appeals to both heart and head, a theology which leads into prayer and a praying which is solidly founded.' *The Tablet*

Praise for *Living Catholicism*

'Particularly compelling is how Strange portrays Jesus as fully human, without compromising the Christian conviction that Jesus was also the son of God. That ability to affirm the faith in its fullness ... without falling back on the ponderous formulations of the dogmatic theologians is one of the more attractive aspects of this work.' *Commonweal*

'*Living Catholicism* is beautifully written: clear, elegant, simple, with enlightening personal anecdotes ... Apart from its style, the spiritual/ doctrinal combination is very effective. Reading it, chapter by chapter, was rather like making a retreat.' Margaret Smart, former Director of the Catholic Education Service

Praise for *The Risk of Discipleship*

'What emerges from the pages of this book is a passionate and convincing awareness of the personal call to pastoral ministry, firmly rooted in the Word of God ... I personally found the chapter on the place of the ordained ministry within the common priesthood of all the baptised particularly apposite for the current situation of the Church ... If I can become more like the sort of priest described in these pages, I will be very content.' Bishop Crispian Hollis, *Priests and People*

'...a luminous and realistic portrait of priesthood.' Lawrence Cunningham

JOHN HENRY NEWMAN:

A Mind Alive

RODERICK STRANGE

DARTON·LONGMAN + TODD

First published in 2008 by
Darton, Longman and Todd Ltd
1 Spencer Court
140 – 142 Wandsworth High Street
London SW18 4JJ

Reprinted 2008, 2009, 2010

ISBN 10: 0-232-52723-7
ISBN 13: 978-0-232-52723-0

A catalogue record for this book is available from the British Library

Typeset by YHT Ltd, London
Printed and bound in Great Britain
by Page Bros, Norwich, Norfolk.

For
Anne-Marie, Gill, and Alison

Contents

Acknowledgements

Some parts of this book have been adapted from earlier articles of mine in *The Ampleforth Journal, The Clergy Review, Priests and People, Louvain Studies, Marian Studies, Newman-Studien, One in Christ, The Canadian Catholic Review*, and from contributions to Perry Butler (ed.), *Pusey Rediscovered*, (London, 1983), Rosario La Delfa and Alessandro Magno (eds.), *Luce nella Solitudine*, (Palermo, 1989), Rosario La Delfa (ed.), *Il Viaggio e La Malattia di Newman in Sicilia*, (Palermo, 1991), and Paul Vaiss (ed.), *Newman: from Oxford to the People*, (Leominster, 1996). The final chapter is based on 'The Flame of Love', which appeared in *Priests and People* in December 1990 and was originally broadcast on BBC Radio 3 on 16 September 1990. I am grateful for permission to make use of this material again here.

Unless stated otherwise, scriptural quotations have been taken from the New Revised Standard Version, Catholic Edition, published by Geoffrey Chapman in 1993, and quotations from the Council documents have been taken from Norman Tanner (ed.), *Decrees of the Ecumenical Councils*, 2 vols., (London and Washington, 1990).

Abbreviations

The abbreviations I have used are those which have become standard and are listed in C. S. Dessain et al. (eds.), *The Letters and Diaries of John Henry Newman* i – xxxii, (Oxford and London, 1961–2008); hereafter *L.D.*

Page references are taken from the Uniform Edition of Newman's works. Where a second reference is given in square brackets, it is taken from a subsequent critical edition, noted below.

Apo.	*Apologia pro Vita Sua*
Ari.	*The Arians of the Fourth Century*
Ath. i, ii	*Select Treatises of St Athanasius*
A.W.	*Autobiographical Writings*
D.A.	*Discussions and Arguments on Various Subjects*
Dev.	*An Essay on the Development of Christian Doctrine*
Diff. i, ii	*Certain Difficulties felt by Anglicans in Catholic Teaching*
Ess. i, ii	*Essays Critical and Historical*
G.A.	*An Essay in aid of a Grammar of Assent*
H.S. i, ii, iii	*Historical Sketches*
Idea	*The Idea of a University defined and illustrated*
Jfc.	*Lectures on the Doctrine of Justification*
M.D.	*Meditations and Devotions of the late Cardinal Newman*
Mix.	*Discourses addressed to Mixed Congregations*
O.S.	*Sermons preached on Various Occasions*
P.S. i-viii	*Parochial and Plain Sermons*
Prepos.	*Present Position of Catholics in England*
S.D.	*Sermons bearing on Subjects of the Day*
T.T.	*Tracts Theological and Ecclesiastical*
U.S.	*Fifteen Sermons preached before the University of Oxford*
V.M. i, ii	*The Via Media*
V.V.	*Verses on Various Occasions*

Critical Editions

Martin J. Svalgic (ed.), *Apologia pro Vita Sua*, (Oxford, 1967)

Ian T. Ker (ed.), *An Essay in aid of a Grammar of Assent*, (Oxford, 1985)

Ian T. Ker (ed.), *The Idea of a University*, (Oxford, 1976)

H. D. Weidner (ed.), *The 'Via Media' of the Anglican Church*, (Oxford, 1990)

Preface

When people are beatified or canonised, they are being offered to us as examples of holiness that we can follow with confidence. We need not suppose, however, that they have always been perfect. John Henry Newman once said as much about one of his theological heroes, St Cyril of Alexandria, who, as a churchman, could be a ruthless political operator. We are not obliged, Newman remarked, to defend aspects of his ecclesiastical career: 'It does not answer to call whity-brown, white' (*H.S.ii.* p. 342). Much more recently, Pope Benedict XVI has echoed that view. In his Wednesday audience on 31 January 2007, he observed that 'the saints have not "fallen from Heaven". They are people like us, who also have complicated problems. Holiness does not consist in never having erred or sinned.'[1] These are comforting words.

Newman himself has been a significant influence in my life. He will soon be beatified. My debt to him is far-reaching. In this book, however, I am not suggesting that he was always right about everything. I do not feel obliged to champion and defend every position he took. 'Holiness does not consist in never having erred or sinned.' All the same, as his cause for beatification makes plain, he has a great deal to offer us.

I myself started to read Newman's work when I was eighteen and I am reading and studying him still. What is more, after my ordination as a Catholic priest, I was given the chance to study his life and thought at some depth while engaged in doctoral research at Oxford. Once that was completed, there were further opportunities: invitations began to arrive to write articles about aspects of

---

1 See *L'Osservatore Romano*, Weekly Edition in English, 7 February 2007, p. 11.

his thought or give lectures on him or contribute chapters to books which were being prepared about him. In this way, over the years, a considerable amount of material has come together. I do not claim that it is startlingly original, but I would like to think that it offers helpful avenues into understanding Newman himself, his ideas, and his approach to problems and difficulties which often enough we still struggle with today. Moreover, the benefits I have received from him are benefits I would wish to share with others. In part that wish has prompted this book.

At the same time, this is not a collection, or even a selection, of my writings on Newman. It draws on them, but it edits, adapts, and re-arranges them. Much of this material is new text, composed for the first time or developed from notes that I have made for lectures and talks over the years. I am writing for people who are curious about Newman and would like to know more, and for those who enjoy reading, but have little time for long books outside their own area of interest or expertise. I would like to think that those who only have time to read one book about Newman will find that this is the one. They may do so in part precisely because they can relate to something personal, Newman's influence on me which I am happy to acknowledge.

It will be obvious, therefore, that this book does not pretend to be exhaustive, resolving disputes of scholarly detail between Newman specialists. Newman wrote so much that he created a rich arena for debate. Those controversies may have something to teach us, but they are not my concern here. I plan rather to offer access to his life and thought and experience by avoiding un-necessary detail. I shall draw attention instead to some of the elements which have impressed me and which may, therefore, still be valuable to others.

I start with those points which made an immediate impact on me at the beginning. Then I sketch his life so as to offer a feel for events, for what happened, especially his search for the Church. That search itself was lifelong. Next, I have tried to offer a map of his mind. This chapter is called 'A Mind Alive', and echoes the sub-title of this book. It is central, but not because Newman can be reduced to an icy intellectual. His mind was alive because it reached out to touch the heart and engage the whole person. That union of mind and heart and person will be evident time and again in what follows. In particular, the mind came alive by recognising the relationship between dogma and theology. Newman championed dogma, the mysteries at the heart of the Church's faith; that is well known. But he championed too the role of theology which by scrutiny tries to keep dogma pure.

That interplay of dogma and theology is illustrated in his interpretation of infallible authority in the Church and evident also in the way he presented teaching about the Blessed Virgin Mary. Then the value he placed on the role of the laity has also been influential. And those issues – infallibility, Mariology, and the laity – reflected his care for ecumenism as well, the need for the Church to be one. These subjects occupy the chapters that follow. After probing them, we can return to the man himself, his awareness of divine providence, his preaching about faith, and his life as a witness to holiness. And at the end, as a kind of coda, there is a reflection on his poem, *The Dream of Gerontius*.

Once again, I wish to record my appreciation and gratitude for the encouragement and wise advice that I have received consistently from Brendan Walsh and Helen Porter at Darton, Longman and Todd. This book is the fourth I have published with them. That fact alone speaks volumes for the support and help that they and their colleagues have offered me in recent years.

Although in preparing this particular text I have not needed to visit Father Paul Chavasse and the Fathers at the Birmingham Oratory, I have clear memories of their generous hospitality when my Newman studies were in their infancy. And whenever I have visited since, they have always received me warmly. I thank them now especially for permission to use the photograph of Newman on the cover and I take this opportunity to pay tribute to Gerard Tracey, who has died, and to Brother Francis McGrath, FMS, for their work in completing the publication of Newman's *Letters and Diaries*, and for the kind assistance they have always been ready to offer me.

I am conscious too of the debts I owe to others who have studied Newman and whose friendship and insight have encouraged me, people like Bishop Geoffrey Rowell, Nicholas Lash, Ian Ker, Sheridan Gilley, Joyce Sugg and Stephen Prickett. There are too many to mention, but no list of mine must omit two who have died, John Coulson and the incomparable Stephen Dessain. And I wish also to thank my friend and colleague at the Beda College, Fr John Breen. Chapter by chapter, as it was completed, was passed before his keen, critical, but non-specialist eye. His help was invaluable. Then over dinner one evening another friend, Father Paul Murray, OP, poet and wise man, suggested the book's title. I am grateful to them both.

And finally, there is the dedication. Newman had three sisters, and so have I. The eldest, Anne-Marie, I never knew for she died at birth, but she is no less loved because of that. And the other two, Gill and Alison, have filled my life with friendship, love, and laughter. I thank them with love. I am proud to dedicate this book to my sisters.

1

'Have you Read any Newman?'

(i)

It was my good fortune when I went up to Oxford in 1970 to study Newman to find that Father Stephen Dessain, that prince among Newman scholars, had agreed to be my supervisor. Stephen was a member of the Birmingham Oratory which Newman had founded. He was deeply devoted to Newman and his knowledge of Newman's writings was without equal. His small biography, *John Henry Newman*, which was first published in 1966, remains the best brief biography of the Cardinal, and the twenty-one volumes of Newman's *Letters and Diaries* which he edited and saw published between 1961 and his death in 1976, bear witness to his grasp of the corpus and his scholarship. Although he assisted countless other people with their research, I was to be his only full-time student.

Stephen and I knew each other a little already from his visits to Rome while I was a student at the English College and he had come to my priestly ordination on 21 December 1969. By chance it was the anniversary of his own. Ever generous, he brought me as a present the collection of Newman's Oratorian papers which had been edited by Dom Placid Murray and published the year before with the title *Newman the Oratorian*.[1] Inside he had written Newman's words about God's hidden saints and their influence: 'Say they are few, such high Christians; and what follows? They are enough to carry on God's noiseless work' (*U.S.* p. 96). While Newman was referring to the saints, I have no doubt that Stephen was thinking of Newman. And this book is in part my attempt to

---

1 Placid Murray, *Newman the Oratorian*, (Dublin, 1969).

explore Newman's influence on me, his part for me in 'God's noiseless work'.

I can date the time and place where it all began precisely. It was the morning of 30 March 1964 and I was in a Roman bus on my way to the Alban Hills, south of the city. It was Easter Monday. I had come to the English College as a seminarian the previous October and that Monday I was going to Palazzola, the College's villa, for a week's break after Easter before lectures began again. I was travelling with Tony Cornish, a fellow student and, since 1967, a priest of the Plymouth Diocese. We were talking about this and that, and then at one point Tony turned to me and asked, 'Have you read any Newman, Rod?' I had not. I had only the vaguest idea who Newman was. I had seen portraits. He then told me about Meriol Trevor's two-volume biography which had been published recently and which the College library had just acquired.[2] When I got back to Rome, I went to find it and decided to read it that summer during our long vacation. And I did.

What I read captivated me. I went on at once to read Newman himself. I began with his *Apologia pro Vita Sua*, in which he gave his account of his journey to Catholicism, and I wrote my own extended summary of it as a way of trying to grasp a little more clearly the sequence of events. It would be fair to say that I have been reading and studying Newman's work ever since. There has been much else, of course, but Newman has never been too far away.

What was it that impressed me? In many ways, as I have said, this entire book is an answer to that question, but let me begin by mentioning three aspects in particular which struck me almost immediately.

---

2 Meriol Trevor, *Newman: the Pillar of the Cloud* (vol. i); *Newman: Light in Winter* (vol. ii), (London, 1962).

(ii)

First, like most people, I love a good story and I found the story of Newman's life enthralling. It revolves around the twin ingredients of controversy and surprise. The young Newman, though shy, was recognised as brilliant. When he took his degree, however, he managed only to scrape a pass. Intensity and overwork had drained him. Nevertheless, the following year he was elected a Fellow of Oriel, which at that time was regarded as the very cream of Oxford intellectual society.

As a College tutor Newman believed that his care for his pupils should extend beyond simply the teaching he gave them. Something more personal, a moral dimension, was needed. Many years later he was to state his view plainly: 'An academical system without the personal influence of teachers upon pupils, is an arctic winter; it will create an ice-bound, petrified, cast-iron University, and nothing else' (*H.S.* iii, p. 74). A view which is commonplace nowadays was seen then as a reform so radical that he had his pupils withdrawn. And one ironical consequence of that action was for him to find himself with time available, when the moment came some years later, to devote himself wholeheartedly to the Oxford Movement which aimed to renew the Church of England by restoring to it its share in the Catholic tradition.

When it began, he was its driving force. But then he found himself drawn by his own arguments and a series of events to doubt the very position for which he was so eloquent an advocate. Some years later, after anguished study and reflection, he ceased being an Anglican and was received into the Roman Catholic Church. That was in 1845. This decision was as painful as it was dramatic, for it caused a parting from friends which only long years and abiding affection on both sides would overcome.

Catholicism, however, was no safe haven for him. Further controversies ensued.

After ordination in Rome, he established the Congregation of the Oratory in Birmingham and London, but later his plans were marred by an unhappy dispute between the two houses. Then during a series of lectures in 1851 he took the opportunity to respond to the scandalous allegations against Catholics which were being made in England by a former Dominican friar, Giacinto Achilli, and he was tried for libel. The evidence which would have cleared him had been mislaid by Cardinal Nicholas Wiseman, the Archbishop of Westminster, and a prejudiced jury found Newman guilty. Many people were outraged and the verdict prompted *The Times* to observe that Roman Catholics could no longer have faith in British justice.

During this time he was also working to found a university in Dublin at the invitation of the Irish bishops, but was consistently being denied the support he needed to make the venture succeed. Then in 1859, the year following his return to England, he was persuaded to accept the editorship of the Catholic periodical, *The Rambler*, which the bishops regarded as too critical; he was judged to be a safer pair of hands and acceptable to both the bishops and the periodical's proprietors. His attempt to calm anxieties, however, misfired and almost at once he was asked to resign. The situation deteriorated further for him because soon afterwards an article of his on consulting the laity brought him under suspicion in Rome. His readiness to answer objections was passed on to the Church authorities; but as the questions they then sent were never passed back to him, he assumed all was well, while they assumed he would not reply. He remained under a cloud for some years.

At the end of 1863 matters came to a head. He was accused by Charles Kingsley of indifference to the truth and there poured out from him his *Apologia pro Vita Sua*. That controversy marked a turning-point, at least with regard to the respect in which he was held by his contemporaries. Yet there were more controversies to follow. His plans for establishing an Oratory in Oxford were encouraged at first, but then frustrated, and notably his moderate interpretation of the doctrine of papal infallibility brought him into conflict with Archbishop (later Cardinal) Manning's extreme ultramontane view. But finally in old age his life became more serene.

In 1878 Trinity College, Oxford, where he had been an undergraduate, invited him to become its first honorary fellow and so he visited Oxford again for the first time in 32 years. And then the following year the new pope, Leo XIII, created him a cardinal. Old wounds were being healed, the cloud was lifted from him for ever.

As a young man, beginning my preparation for ministerial priesthood, it seemed to me a stirring tale, an example of love for the truth and fidelity to Christ and the Church, and it compelled my admiration.

A second aspect which caught my attention was the fact that Newman was English. It may help to remember that, when I began reading him, the Second Vatican Council was in progress. The Council was encouraging a growing awareness of the local church, and Newman's personality and his approach to many issues gave a clear example of what that could mean for England. The point is not chauvinistic. His influence in other countries is too well known for that. It is simply a matter of acknowledging that when the Church in Council was trying to recognise what each culture could contribute to its life, Newman supplied a particular illustration of what the English contribution might be. On one occasion years later some friends who were not Catholics were joking with me by saying that Newman had never really been a Catholic, but was always an Anglican at heart. I responded by saying that on the contrary I felt Newman had shown how being English and a Catholic were compatible. It was just banter, but I may have struck a nerve, because there was a sudden silence and the subject was changed.

Thinking of banter, it is perhaps worth adding here that people don't usually associate Newman with humour. But I found that preconception mistaken. Let me offer examples.

On holiday in the Mediterranean in 1832, there is a splendidly comic account of his seasickness: 'the worst of seasickness', he observed in a long letter to his mother on 23 December, 'is the sympathy which all things on board have with the illness, as if they were seasick too.' He goes on to describe the movement of table and chairs – swing, swing – and the motion of the glasses, knives and forks on the tables, with wine spilling – swing, swing – and trying to hide the misery you are feeling, until you can do so no longer, but when you get up, you can't move, because the ship is moving, and when you finally make your berth, the door won't shut, then 'bang, bang, you slam your fingers'. Then, when you lie down, there is the noise of the bulkheads, the noises of the gale, 'creaking, clattering, shivering, and dashing', not to mention the bilge water, which he calls an 'unspeakable nuisance', set in motion by the storm and draining down to the bottom of the boat (*L.D.* iii, p. 159). The whole passage is masterly. And his letters generally are full of comic observation, such as his comment on William Wilberforce's false teeth, and his habit of throwing 'the whole set out of the gums upon his tongue, and [chewing] them, as an infant might a coral' (*L.D.* xx, p. 261). And there is the story of Newman laughing, just before sending off the final proofs of *A Grammar of Assent* which he had dedicated to his friend, Edward Bellasis, 'in remembrance of a long, equable, sunny friendship'. Just in time he noticed that the dedication recalled instead 'a long, equable, funny friendship'. There is plenty more.[3]

And a third element which impressed me early on was Newman's instinct for pastoral care. I soon discovered that when people knew anything about him at all, they tended to think in stereotypes, contrasting him with his contemporary, Cardinal Henry Edward Manning. Manning was seen as the practical one, involved in the world's affairs, while Newman was regarded as intellectual and remote.[4] But the reality was very different. I was struck by Newman's practicality, his commitment to pastoral matters and the administrative skill that went with it.

When he took up his first curacy at St Clement's in Oxford, he was an earnest evangelical Anglican, who, while not believing in predestination, was convinced that more people were damned than were saved. But by caring for his parishioners, he learnt

3 See Trevor, *Newman: Light in Winter*, p. 486. For more on this theme, see Joyce Sugg, 'Did Newman Have a Sense of Humour?', *The Clergy Review* lxviii (1983) 100–5.

4 To correct the caricature, see David Newsome, *The Convert Cardinals: Newman and Manning*, (London, 1993).

otherwise. How could the majority of such good people be destined for hell? he wondered; that could not be true. Then, as I noted earlier, when he became a tutor at Oriel, he could not see that role as a matter merely of intellectual instruction. And later as vicar of the University Church and leader of the Oxford Movement, he was full of pastoral energy. His preaching from that time has become legendary. 'It is of the essence of the Movement,' Owen Chadwick has observed, 'that its best writing should be enshrined in parochial sermons.'[5]

After his reception into full communion with the Catholic Church in 1845 the same energy drove him on. He established the Oratories in Birmingham and London and founded the Catholic University in Dublin. He also set up the Oratory School. In all these projects, his administrative gifts as well as his pastoral instinct were fully engaged. That pastoral instinct was also evident decisively in his vast correspondence with an astonishing range of people and found further expression in his other writings where his devotion to what was real, as he would say, rather than the merely notional was always evident. He had no time for theories, however splendid, if they could make no impact. 'I say plainly I do not want to be converted by a smart syllogism;' he wrote in *A Grammar of Assent* which he published in 1870, 'if I am asked to convert others by it I say plainly I do not care to overcome their reason without touching their hearts' (*G.A.* p. 425 [273]).

Such pastoral commitment could hardly fail to inspire me as a young man as my own preparation for ministerial priesthood gathered momentum. And then there was something else, something interior.

(iii)

Effective pastoral work needs to be more than activity. It must be in tune with the man within; it must flow from spirituality. Reading Newman I soon became aware of his extraordinarily

5 Owen Chadwick, *The Mind of the Oxford Movement*, (London, 1960), p. 42.

vivid sense of God's existence and presence. His pastoral instinct and energy were undeniable; in no way was he in flight from practical demands; nevertheless, it could be said that there was a sense for him in which the unseen world had a greater reality than the seen. Early in his *Apologia* he described himself as coming to rest when young 'in the thought of two and two only absolute and luminously self-evident beings, myself and my Creator' (*Apo*. p. 4 [18]). In other words, he was as sure of God's existence as he was of his own. Few of us would probably be able to make such a claim, or at least we would not make it in those terms. All the same, it is wonderful to be encouraged, as I was by Newman at that time, as I prepared myself for priestly ministry, to look beyond the visible world and nurture a sense of the world unseen. Sensitivity to the unseen stimulates that longing for God which is indispensable for a life of prayer.

Styles and approaches in prayer are very varied. Some people love the company of others when they pray, and the stimulus of words and music. My usual preference would be for stillness. One image of Newman's has never failed to help me. In a sermon called 'Equanimity' he asks: 'Did you ever look at an expanse of water, and observe the ripples on the surface? Do you think that disturbance penetrates below it?' He goes on to speak of tempests and scenes of horror and distress at sea, but remarks, 'The foundations of the ocean, the vast realms of water which girdle the earth, are as tranquil and as silent in the storm as in a calm.' He uses it as an image for the souls of those who are holy: 'They have a well of peace springing up within them unfathomable' (*P.S.* v, p. 69). As the passage continues, he acknowledges how troubled we may sometimes be in fact, and indeed the tsunami at Christmas 2004 may seem to qualify the image further; but that tragic event cannot simply cancel it altogether. The appeal to tranquillity in the deep has given me encouragement to persevere in prayer beyond immediate difficulties in order to discover the strength and stillness of God.

Hand in hand with this belief in God's existence and presence and the call to prayerfulness went Newman's sense of God's providence: the Lord is not only close to us; he cares for us. No one can read Newman's life carefully and believe he thought otherwise. The idea may seem bewildering to many people today, implying divine intrusion into the natural course of events, or their manipulation. But that was not how Newman saw it. He believed that God has a plan for each of us, a plan made real by his presence abiding amongst us, a plan and a presence which we see as providential when we recognise the divine presence within the events that are taking place. We call providential those moments or occasions in our lives when we become aware of God's will for us. They are privileged perceptions of his abiding presence.

It took a long while for my own appreciation of providence to reach this stage, but I remember clearly how it began. I was reading one of Newman's sermons and came to these words: 'God beholds thee individually, whoever thou art. He "calls thee by thy name". He sees thee and understands thee, as He made thee.' And so it went on, concluding, 'Thou dost not love thyself better than He loves thee' (*PS.* iii, pp. 124–5). If time has mellowed the initial impact of those words, it has not diminished their reality for me. We can explore Newman's understanding of providence more fully later.[6]

Fascination with the English Newman's long life and his pastoral instinct, on the one hand, and his profound spirituality, on the other, have had their influence on me. Before continuing further, however, let me mention one other way, specific and practical, in which I have found myself following his example over the years.

(iv)

When Newman published the first volume of his *Parochial Sermons* in 1834, the custom was to include in some way the whole range of Christian doctrine, but he was criticised because he had placed emphasis on some aspects of the Church's teaching and ignored others. His friend, Samuel Wilberforce, took him to task. He wrote to complain that Newman was too severe in his demands for

6 See below, pp. 109–22.

an evident change of heart, and that he had not made sufficient allowance for the work of the Spirit in bringing sinners to repentance. But Newman remained unmoved. It is not necessary to go into the details of that controversy here. It is enough to recognise that Newman was not intending to deny the power of the Spirit working in people; however, he felt the need at that time to bring out the importance of an individual's response to grace. That was the aspect he wished to emphasise. There would be opportunities for other aspects at other times. And the particular point that impressed me was his assertion that he could not deal with everything at once. As he told Wilberforce: 'I lay it down as a fundamental Canon, that a Sermon to be effective must be imperfect.' He could not bring in every doctrine everywhere. At one time certain elements would be considered, at another time others. However, he claimed, 'No one, who *habitually* hears me, ought to have any other than the whole Scripture impression' (*L.D.* v, p. 38). The plan was to proceed part by part; the result would be an account of the whole. Working in very different circumstances, that is precisely what I have tried to do.

Both as a priest in a parish and particularly as a university chaplain, I have sought to supply a whole account of the Church's teaching. It has not generally been practicable to do so by offering a series of extended lectures. Instead it has had to be done gradually, through homilies and talks, assembling little by little the pieces of the jigsaw. And there is evidence of the outcome. In 1986 I published a small book. Called *The Catholic Faith*, it was essentially a reworking into a whole of homilies and sermons, lectures and talks, which I had been giving at the Oxford University Chaplaincy. It treats of Christ and the Church, the sacraments and the virtues, Mary and the Trinity. A later book, *Living Catholicism*, published in 2001, emerged in much the same way. They have generally been well received, and the material in them was gathered by following Newman's approach.[7]

7 See Roderick Strange, *The Catholic Faith*, (Oxford, 1986, reprinted London, 2001); and *idem. Living Catholicism*, (London, 2001).

(v)

Many other aspects of Newman's life, like the valuing of friends, and of his thought, like the role of theological reflection, and of his experience, like love and care for the unity of the Church, have made their mark on me over the years. They will become evident as this book unfolds. And there have, of course, been other influences besides Newman, some of them no doubt qualifying and adapting what I have learnt from him, but it would be dishonest of me to disclaim the impact he has had on my life and priestly ministry.

Some years after I had been ordained and while I was studying him in Oxford as a graduate priest, a friend asked me why I did not quote him more often when I preached. The question took me by surprise and I had to think carefully to find the answer. Then I realised that in fact I was quoting him frequently, but rarely word for word. His influence goes deeper. My debt is incalculable, my gratitude profound.

2

Newman's Path

(i)

Newman was born on 21 February 1801 and died on 11 August 1890. It was a long and involved life, profound and complex. In October 1963, when Pope Paul VI was beatifying the Passionist priest, Dominic Barberi, who had received Newman into the Catholic Church, he paused in his address to speak of Newman directly. He described him as someone who 'in full consciousness of his mission – "I have a work to do" – and guided solely by love of the truth and fidelity to Christ, traced an itinerary, the most toilsome, but also the greatest, the most meaningful, the most conclusive, that human thought ever travelled during the [nineteenth] century, indeed one might say during the modern era, to arrive at the fullness of wisdom and of peace'.[1] These words are highly charged. Stephen Dessain remarked to me later that it sounded as though the Pope were beatifying Newman rather than Dominic. Be that as it may, he was clearly aware of Newman's journey.

It is not easy to follow the path of so full a life, but a sketch is needed to provide some context for the issues to be considered later. Various approaches are possible.

I have mentioned already my early fascination with the contrasts in Newman's life, the pattern of expectation and disappointment: the brilliant undergraduate who scarcely manages to get a degree; the tutor at Oriel who has his pupils withdrawn; the leader of the Oxford Movement who becomes a Roman Catholic; the

---

1 See feast of Blessed Dominic Barberi, National Calendar of England and Wales, *The Divine Office* iii, p. 435*.

distinguished convert who is not trusted fully and whose talents are misused; then finally, the unexpected years as a Cardinal, when the cloud is lifted and he is valued and treated with respect. Throughout all that time, Newman was in search of the Church. For him the guiding question was, where was the Body of Christ to be found most fully? He wished to be a member. And when he felt he had answered that question and then had acted upon it, becoming a Catholic in 1845, there were still long years to be lived of maturing, suffering, and humiliation.

There are, perhaps, three main stages to this intriguing life. Until 1833, he was in search of himself; the years from 1833 to 1845 were for him a kind of crucible; after that, the consequences of his decision to become a Catholic were played out.

(ii)

When people speak of Newman's conversion, they are usually referring to the events of 8 and 9 October 1845, that windswept night when Father Dominic Barberi, drenched by rain from his journey exposed to the weather, arrived in Littlemore, the village where Newman had made his home after resigning as Vicar of the University Church and retiring to lay communion as an Anglican. He began to hear Newman's confession that evening and it continued the following morning. Then he received him into the Roman Catholic Church. That conversion, however, had been preceded by others.

Newman had been brought up as a normally devout Anglican who read his Bible and knew it well. In 1816, however, when he was fifteen, while he was at school, he became ill, the first of three significant illnesses of these early years. While recovering, he was given a number of Calvinist books and had an experience of conversion. He believed he was 'elected to eternal glory'. It was the time when he came to rest in 'the thought of two and two only absolute and luminously self-evident beings, myself and my Creator' (*Apo.* p. 4 [17–18]). Nothing dramatic seems to have occurred outwardly; there was nothing wildly enthusiastic that could be likened to baptism in the Spirit or speaking in tongues; but the immediate effects of that experience remained for a while and then faded over a period of about five years. It made Newman earnestly evangelical. That was the young man who went up to Trinity as an undergraduate later the following year.

He was expected to do brilliantly when he came to take his degree in 1820, but in the event it was a disaster. He had over-worked, become over-tired and tense. As he recorded much later, he 'lost his head, utterly broke down, and after vain attempts for several days had to retire'. He secured his degree, but only just. He had failed altogether in mathematics, which was his best subject, and only managed to scrape through in classics (see *A.W.* p. 47).

What was he to do next? His poor degree made the legal career that he had considered seem impossible and he decided to be ordained instead. In due course, he became an Anglican deacon in 1824 and a priest the following year. But, in the meantime, in spite of his poor degree, he had made up his mind to stand for a fel-lowship at Oriel, then the most intellectually prestigious of the Oxford colleges. He was successful and was elected on 12 April 1822. It was not so much the quality of his papers that swayed the electors, but the character of his scholarship. More than twenty years later, Edward Copleston, who had been Provost of Oriel at the time, recalled it, describing Newman as 'not even a good classical scholar, yet in mind and powers of composition, and in taste and knowledge, . . . decidedly superior' to other competitors who had previously gained better degrees as undergraduates (see *A.W.* p. 64). And so Newman found himself a Fellow of Oriel and familiar with some of the most distinguished men in Oxford at that time.

One of them was Richard Whately, who was to become the Archbishop of Dublin in the Church of Ireland. He was colourful in dress, witty in speech, and trenchant in argument. He was also renowned, in Newman's words much later, as 'singularly gracious to undergraduates and young masters' (*A.W.* p. 66). He took Newman under his wing and was the ideal person for bringing the reserved young man out of his shell. Newman was a great listener and Whately a great talker. Moreover, Whately liked to talk logic and he, perhaps more than anyone, helped Newman develop his own formidable forensic skill. Samuel Taylor Coleridge, famous for his *Rime of the Ancient Mariner*, once remarked in his table talk, 'Every man is born an Aristotelian, or a Platonist. I do not think it possible that any one born an Aristotelian can become a Platonist; and I am sure no born Platonist can change into an Aristotelian.'[2] The historian, David Newsome, has suggested, however, that, if there is an exception to Coleridge's dictum, then it is Newman, 'born a Platonist', but through his education 'become an Aristotelian'.[3] And if Newsome is right, then Whately more than anyone else was responsible for helping him learn how the vision whole could be divided into parts.

Subsequent events made Newman and Whately drift apart, but they were close for about ten years. During the earlier years in particular, Newman relished the atmosphere of the Oriel Senior Common Room which was said to 'stink of logic'. It is easy to imagine him, roused from his shyness, becoming aware of his intellectual gifts and taking delight in using them. What could be more natural? This was the time when he fell under the spell of intellectual excellence. That reigned supreme. But its influence did not last. Three factors combined to change his attitude.

First, he became unwell again. Overwork, family worries, College business, and examining responsibilities caused him to collapse while examining in November 1827. Then a few weeks later, on 5 January 1828, his youngest sister, Mary, whom he loved tenderly, died suddenly. Her death shattered him. It is easy to understand why: to read her letters, light but perceptive, humorous and loving, is to realise how lovable she must have been (see *L.D.* ii, pp. 38–9). His own ill-health, therefore, and Mary's death forced him to take stock. What really mattered? How could intellectual excellence compare with the loss of a beloved sister, or

---

2 See H. J. Jackson (ed.), *Samuel Taylor Coleridge*, (Oxford, 1985), pp. 594–5.

3 See David Newsome, *Two Classes of Men: Platonism and English Romantic Thought*, (London, 1974), p. 72.

even to damage to his own good health? And at that very time other Oriel friendships were developing, drawing him away from Whately. In particular he was coming to know Edward Pusey who was studious, John Keble who was saintly, and more immediately Hurrell Froude who was irrepressible, but was to die prematurely from consumption in 1836. Their influence would grow and he would come increasingly to share with them devotion to the Catholic tradition within the Church of England which was to be fundamental to the Oxford Movement. Here was another conversion. He was no longer dazzled by the intellect in isolation. In so far as he could be said to have flirted with rationalism, the flirtation was over.

The College business which had preoccupied Newman when he was taken ill in 1827 was the need to elect a new Provost, a new head of House for Oriel. When the time came, Newman voted for Edward Hawkins who was in fact elected. He had been kind to Newman when he first became a Fellow. And Hawkins is in a way pivotal at this stage of Newman's life.

In the first place, it was through Hawkins that Newman had come to an understanding of baptism as new birth, independent of personal experience, and so had been helped to shed his earlier severe evangelicalism; and, listening to Hawkins when he was an undergraduate, he had begun to learn from him the significance of tradition. Then secondly, Hawkins had been the Vicar of St Mary the Virgin, the University Church, but, when he became Provost, he had had to resign. Newman succeeded him and gained thereby a place of influence. It was from the pulpit of St Mary's that he was to deliver some of his most memorable sermons. And finally, it was Hawkins who was opposed to Newman's view of a tutor's duties and, as Provost, opposed that view successfully. And so it was that, when the Oxford Movement began, Newman found he had the time and freedom at his disposal to commit himself to its cause without reserve. In his *Apologia*, while Newman acknowledged their differences, he also declared his abiding affection for Hawkins personally. And Hawkins wrote a kind letter, thanking him (see *Apo.* pp. 8–10 [21–2; 485–6]).

In 1832, however, deprived of pupils and, therefore, without teaching responsibilities, Newman was able to take a holiday. He went with Hurrell Froude, who by that time was already starting to sicken with the consumption that would eventually kill him, and with Archdeacon Froude, Hurrell's father, on a Mediterranean holiday. They toured widely, including, for Newman, a first visit to Rome where they called in at the English College and met Nicholas Wiseman who was then the Rector and who would later become a Cardinal and the first Archbishop of Westminster. Newman was fascinated by the whole experience, but questioning. He wrote many poems during this holiday. One begins:

> O that thy creed were sound!
> For thou dost soothe the heart, thou Church of Rome,
> By thy unwearied watch and varied round
> Of service, in thy Saviour's holy home. (*V. V.* p. 153)

Most of all, however, he loved Sicily. He had visited it with the Froudes before going on to Rome and been enchanted by it. So, when they were set to continue their journey towards England, he changed his plans, left them, and returned to visit the island once more. There he fell ill again, the third major illness of these early years. He felt guilty. He saw it as a punishment for his wilfulness, selfishly deserting his friends to follow his own desire. Indeed, he might have died. But in his sickness he was also overcome by a sense of mission, 'I have a work to do', words recalled by Pope Paul when he was beatifying Dominic Barberi. He recovered and set off for England. Becalmed in the Straits of Bonifacio on 16 June 1833, he composed his poem, 'The Pillar of the Cloud', which is better known now as the hymn, 'Lead, Kindly Light'. In it he acknowledges the darkness and his own pride, but trusts in the power that has blessed him and will lead him on, 'o'er moor and fen, o'er crag and torrent, till the night is gone' (*V. V.* pp. 156–7). He arrived back in England on 8 July.

These early years, marked by maturing views, from evangelicalism through a kind of rationalism to a more harmonious sense of

the Church of England as also Catholic, and scarred by personal
crisis, sickness and death, had brought Newman to a turning-
point. He had sensed it while he was ill in Sicily: there was a work
to do. Then, six days after his return, on 14 July 1833, John Keble
preached the Assize Sermon in Oxford.

(iii)

For Newman that sermon signalled the start of the Oxford
Movement, but in fact events were less clear-cut. For some time
there had been those in the Church of England who were afraid
that the Church would come to be controlled by the State. How
then could it be free to proclaim the Gospel, should conflict arise?
And conflict, they felt, had now arisen. The issue, soon forgotten
in itself, was Parliament's re-ordering of the Church in Ireland
through the suppression of some dioceses. In practice, it was an
entirely sensible matter; in principle, however, it was seen as
undermining the independence of the Church, the State inter-
fering with the successors of the apostles. Keble's sermon, entitled
'National Apostasy', became a trigger for action.

Some gathered at Hadleigh parsonage in Suffolk and discussed
the forming of committees around the country that would help
spread Catholic principles within the Anglican Church. Newman
did not attend the meeting and was impatient with the outcome.
'Living movements do not come of committees', he remarked in
his *Apologia*, and with others he set about writing brief articles
instead, summoning the Church of England to an understanding of
itself based on Catholic principles (see *Apo.* p. 39 [46]). These were
the tracts that gave the Oxford Movement its other name, Tractarian. In the beginning he had them printed himself and he rode
around the countryside from parsonage to parsonage distributing
them. Later they became much longer, but in the beginning they
were leaflets.

Fundamental to the Oxford Movement was care for the
integrity of the Church. That was the cause which Newman was
championing. He had no doubt that the Church of England was a

branch of the great Church Catholic, Roman, Eastern, and Anglican, but he saw it under threat from evangelicals and liberals and from High and Dry Churchmen who had lost a sense of its rich heritage.

To remedy that loss he gave his own account of the Anglican Church. He presented it as a *via media*, a middle way, between Roman excess, on the one hand, and Protestant error, on the other. He distilled his approach in a series of lectures which he delivered in St Mary's and then published in 1837. These were his *Lectures on the Prophetical Office of the Church*. The core of his position rested on three fundamental convictions.

First, he described the Church as indefectible, but not infallible. Infallibility, he argued, was characteristic of the Church united, but since it had been scarred by division, that promise had been lost. Nevertheless, the Church is guided divinely to teach essential, saving truth indefectibly (see *V.M.* i, pp. 201, 190 [228, 219]). Secondly, to identify that truth he appealed to antiquity, to the Scriptures and the Church of the Fathers, to that teaching that had been taught always, everywhere, and by all, '*quod semper, quod ubique, quod ab omnibus*', as the Creed for admission and as the rule of teaching subsequently (see *V.M.* i, p. 222 [245]). And, thirdly, he drew out the way this essential Gospel teaching had been handed down in the Creed from bishop to bishop and so was called Episcopal tradition, while there was also another vast, less formal tradition, 'pervading the Church like an atmosphere', which interprets revelation and unfolds its mysteries; this tradition he called prophetical (see *V.M.* i, pp. 249–51 [267–9]). That, in brief, was the basis of the understanding of the Church which Newman advocated. Even at the outset he was aware of a weakness: while 'Popery and Protestantism are real religions', he observed, ' . . . the *Via Media*, viewed as an integral system, has never had existence except on paper' (*V.M.* i, p. 16 [70–1]). Nevertheless, for six years, in spite of gruelling controversy, all was well. He championed his cause under a cloudless sky. Then a cloud appeared.

Newman valued precedents. Present integrity was secure because it was reflected in the past. During the long vacation in

1839, however, while he was reading at leisure, studying the history of Monophysitism, a fifth-century heresy, he suddenly became alarmed. The Monophysite understanding of Christ, that in Christ there was only one nature, the divine, had been condemned. At the same time, the Monophysites themselves had remained utterly opposed to the Eutychians, whose account of the one divine nature in Christ was more extreme than theirs. What caused Newman alarm was not this understanding of Christ; he had no sympathy with the Monophysites. What alarmed him was the lesson the controversy suggested about the Church. He saw the extremists, the Eutychians, as Protestants. Rome, safeguarding the faith, was the same then as now. Where were the Monophysites? They were in the middle way. They may have resisted the extreme Eutychian view, but their compromising *via media* had also been condemned. 'I saw my face in [a] mirror,' Newman explained in his *Apologia*, 'and I was a Monophysite' (*Apo*. p. 114 [108]). His standpoint seemed fatally flawed, the past undid the present.

Then someone gave him an article by Nicholas Wiseman on the Anglican claim to apostolic succession. The article made little impression at first, but later a friend pointed out to him a phrase of St Augustine's which he had passed over before, '*Securus judicat orbis terrarum*'. The words almost defy translation, but Newman's version was, 'The universal Church is in its judgments secure of truth' (*Ess*. ii, p. 101). The very idea overwhelmed him. He did not, because of it, suppose that the majority was always right; sometimes the few had to withstand the many. But by those words, he later recorded, words which interpreted and summed up the long and varied course of the Church's history, 'the theory of the *Via Media* was absolutely pulverized' (*Apo*. p. 117 [110–11]). He felt as though he had seen a ghost and the thought flashed through his mind, 'The Church of Rome will be found right after all'; then it vanished (see *Apo*. p. 118 [111]).

What happened next was what happens frequently when people are busy. Newman returned to work and the impact of his summer reading gradually faded. For two more years there was calm. But then the ghost returned.

In 1841, while beginning again his study of fourth-century Arianism, he found the earlier pattern recurring. This time it was the Arians who were like Protestants, Rome remaining the same, and the Anglican middle way, the *via media*, so far as it existed, was the path taken by the semi-Arians. Rightly or wrongly, that was how he saw it (see *Apo*. p. 139 [130]). And then in quick succession two further blows fell.

Earlier in the year he had been working on a new tract, No. 90. It contained his reflections on some of the Thirty-Nine Articles, showing how they could be interpreted in a way that was compatible with the teaching of the Council of Trent. The line, of course, was controversial. The Articles were regarded by Anglicans as a bulwark against Popery, Romanism and superstition. But Newman wanted to show that, as the Articles had been drawn up as part of the Elizabethan Settlement 'with the purpose of including Catholics', of helping them feel at home in the Church of England, 'Catholics now will not be excluded' (see *V.M.* ii, p. 348). His motive in writing was to restrain some younger, headstrong Tractarians who were eager to desert the Church of England and become Roman Catholics. He anticipated trouble, but not much. He felt people were becoming bored with Tractarianism; it was no longer attracting much attention; perhaps two or three bishops might object. He was mistaken. For the next three years bishop after bishop condemned the Tract, twenty-four of them in all. He was stunned. It was not merely the ferocity of the onslaught. Episcopal authority lay at the heart of the Tractarian understanding of the Church, obedience to it at the heart of the Tractarian disposition. Yet here were the bishops using the status he had championed for them, condemning a position he believed was inescapable. Where could he turn? He was at a loss. He could not become a Protestant. Clinging to the Church of England, reluctant to go to Rome, he wanted to follow reason, not be a victim of his emotions. Then a second blow fell, confirming the first.

A decision was taken to establish a Bishopric in Jerusalem. The idea came originally from the Prussians, but was supported in England by the Archbishop of Canterbury among others. It was intended to give Protestants a centre in the Holy Land, and the intention was for the bishop to be alternately Anglican and Lutheran or Calvinist. Newman recoiled from the notion. He was committed to an understanding of the Church of England as distinct from Protestantism, a distinction lost on the Anglican supporters of this scheme. They were abandoning the middle way and identifying themselves as a Protestant denomination.

His patristic studies, on the one hand, and these two crises, on the other, brought Newman low. In his own words, he was 'on his death-bed' as an Anglican (_Apo._ p. 147 [137]), but he had not yet died. What was he to do? Where was he to go? Where was the true Church to be found? He had no faith in Protestantism and he could no longer see the Church of England as a path between Protestant error and Roman excess. Only one possibility seemed to remain: could it be that what he had dismissed as Roman corruption was in fact evidence of authentic development? He turned increasingly, therefore, to study the theory of doctrinal development, regarding it as 'a hypothesis to account for a difficulty' (_Dev._ p. 30). He did not hurry. He pursued the question for four more years. Then, in due course, he gathered his findings into his _Essay on the Development of Christian Doctrine_.

The debate, detailed and particular, which his _Essay_ provoked, has been immense and it still goes on. It cannot be resolved here. The drift of Newman's thought, however, may be indicated by an image and by the _Essay's_ most remembered sentence. The image is the image of a stream, which, he noticed, is sometimes said to be 'clearest near the spring': things are purest where they begin. But then he observed: 'Whatever use may fairly be made of this image, it does not apply to the history of a philosophy or belief, which on the contrary is more equable, and purer, and stronger, when its bed has become deep, and broad, and full.' And he drew out his meaning at some length before concluding with the sentence which has been quoted frequently, if not always accurately: 'In a higher world it is otherwise, but here below to live is to change, and to be perfect is to have changed often' (*Dev.* p. 40).

He took his time over the *Essay*, but before it had been completed properly, his mind was made up. On that rainy, windswept night in October, 1845, Dominic Barberi arrived and he was received into the Catholic Church.

(iv)

Newman concluded his *Essay on Development* by speaking of the Catholic Church as the 'Blessed Vision of Peace' (*Dev.* p. 445), and it is true that in one sense his search had come to an end. There were to be no more changes like the ones we have noticed already, from evangelical conversion to the prizing of intellectual excellence to Anglo-Catholicism. And in the early years there was even a kind of honeymoon period, when he displayed at times something like the enthusiasm of the neophyte. He went to Rome to prepare for priestly ordination and was ordained as an Oratorian, returning to England to establish the Oratory there. The Oratorians, founded in Rome by St Philip Neri in the sixteenth century, were secular priests, who lived in community. In a way they resembled at that time the senior common room of an Oxford college. It was an ideal setting for Newman. But the honeymoon did not last. Soon he had to endure, for years, difficulties that drained him, public disgrace, obstruction, frustration, misunderstanding and deceit. In his Journal much later, written in January 1863, he was to remark, 'as a Protestant, I felt my religion dreary, but not my life – but, as a Catholic, my life dreary, not my religion' (*A.W.* p. 254).

The public disgrace was the Achilli trial. While lecturing on Catholicism in England in 1851, Newman took the opportunity to denounce Giacinto Achilli, a former Dominican, who had come to England and was attacking Catholicism on behalf of the Evangelical Alliance. Newman's allegations, exposing Achilli as a liar and sexual predator, merely repeated those already documented in an article by Cardinal Wiseman, so he believed he had the evidence to hand to back his charges. But Achilli, confident that the charges could not be proved, denied them and sued for libel. Wiseman, slow and disorganised, could not find the necessary papers in time and so the matter went to trial. One of Newman's indefatigable friends, Maria Giberne, set off for Italy to track down women whom Achilli had assaulted years previously to persuade them to come to England and give evidence on Newman's behalf. Many were now respectable wives and mothers who had no wish to relive sordid, humiliating incidents from the past, but some were persuaded to come. Nevertheless, the jury found Newman guilty, his charges considered unproven. But the trial judge, Lord Campbell, the Lord Chief Justice, was criticised for his prejudiced handling of the trial and, when the time came for sentence to be passed, Newman's counsel asked for a second trial. There was consternation. In the event the request was denied, but, instead of imprisonment, which he had expected, Newman was lectured on his own moral deterioration since becoming a Catholic and fined £100. The whole episode had hung over him for eighteen months and, although he had won a moral victory, in general he was regarded as disgraced.

While the Achilli drama was unfolding, Newman had been contacted by the Irish bishops in 1851 with a view to his becoming Rector of a new Catholic University in Ireland. Newman eventually agreed and spent a great deal of time and energy on the project for the next seven years. This period was to produce his classic work, *The Idea of a University*. Beside that, however, it brought him only hard labour and anxiety. In brief, there was a clash of viewpoint. While he had in mind a university reflecting the breadth of approach found at Oxford, the bishops wanted something far more limited, little more than a Catholic college. There were tensions among the bishops themselves who were also suspicious of him; and Archbishop Paul Cullen of Dublin, who had first invited Newman to come, exasperated him, ignoring his urgent enquiries and then making decisions without informing him. Needed at his Oratory in Birmingham and ground down by the obstacles that had been placed in his way, he resigned in 1858.

A further difficulty had already begun. In 1857 he was asked by the English bishops to oversee a new translation of the Bible. He felt honoured. He made inquiries and drew up plans, engaging a list of contributors. He was also told that the American bishops were already engaged on a similar project. Contact with the Americans was thrown entirely on to him and then he waited for further instructions, but after December 1858 he heard nothing more. The scheme evaporated. His efforts had been frustrated.

Then within months he was in the thick of the *Rambler* affair. *The Rambler* was a well-regarded Catholic periodical which was at times critical of episcopal action. There were bishops who wished to censure it, and to avoid that Newman's bishop, William Ullathorne, asked him in February 1859 to persuade the editor, Richard Simpson, to resign. Then shortly afterwards Ullathorne approached him again and asked him to take on the editorship himself. Newman, although hesitant at first, eventually agreed to do so, because he supported the basic purpose of *The Rambler* as a periodical for educated lay people. The idea which he still advocated, however, that the laity might have something significant to contribute to the healthy life of the Church was a step too far at that time. Visiting Newman again in May, Ullathorne now suggested that he resign, although he had scarcely begun. All the same, there was one final edition which Newman was still obliged to produce and he decided to use the opportunity to speak about the laity's role. And so he wrote his article, *On Consulting the Faithful in Matters of Doctrine*. It has become renowned. But those opposed to his views attacked him in Rome. When he heard, he sent a letter, offering to show that what he had written was consistent with Church teaching, and in Rome a list of objections was drawn up for his reply. For some reason this list, entrusted to Cardinal Wiseman, was never passed on to him. As he heard nothing, he thought the matter had been dropped, while Rome assumed he was unwilling to answer. Misunderstanding bred suspicion and he remained under a cloud in Rome for the next eight years. Only when some friends visited the Vatican in 1867 was the matter finally clarified and resolved.

Constant adversity, blow after blow, public disgrace, episcopal obstruction, frustration and misunderstanding reduced him to silence. By 1863 he was at a low ebb. Throughout his life he had tried to follow the truth wherever it had led him, at whatever cost, and he had suffered for it. And then he was attacked again. Just before the new year he was sent a copy of *Macmillan's Magazine* for January 1864. In a book review Charles Kingsley, Anglican clergyman, Professor of Modern History at Cambridge, and novelist, remarked in passing,

> Truth, for its own sake, had never been a virtue with the Roman clergy. Father Newman informs us that it need not, and on the whole ought not to be; that cunning is the weapon which heaven has given to the Saints wherewith to withstand the brute male force of the wicked world which marries and is given in marriage. Whether his notion be doctrinally correct or not, it is at least historically so.

Newman stirred. Letters were exchanged with *Macmillan's* publisher and with Kingsley, but he found them unsatisfactory. He realised that the answer to the charge laid against him would never come from controversy alone, a trading of arguments. In any case, it was his truthfulness, his handling of arguments, that was under attack. So he decided to set out the history of his religious opinions. This was his *Apologia pro Vita Sua*. People need not agree with him or be persuaded by the views he held, but at least they might come to see that he had behaved with integrity and held his views honestly. And, moreover, in giving his account, he was able to pay tribute to old friends, to acknowledge what he owed them, and to express his enduring affection for them. What he wrote, reliving the sorrows and separations of the past, caused him acute pain, but it was received and welcomed warmly almost without exception. After nearly twenty years many friendships were restored, his gifts came to be recognised, and his influence once more began to grow.

All the same, there were further hardships to be faced. The most obvious difficulty revolved around the plan for him to establish an Oratorian mission in Oxford. Many English Catholics supported the idea. They wanted their sons to go up to the University in spite of the disapproval of Church authorities, and they regarded Newman as the ideal person to be there to give them pastoral care. Bishop Ullathorne also supported the initiative. Newman obeyed his Bishop and started to plan, finding a site, raising money. But those Catholics who opposed the idea, because they regarded Oxford as anti-Catholic, were fiercely opposed to Newman's presence. They feared that, once he was there, he would act like a magnet, and even more of the young would be attracted to the University. These opponents, notably Henry Manning, the new Archbishop of Westminster, who had once been his friend, were influential, especially in Rome. And so a condition for establishing the Oratory was laid down, but hidden from Newman: Newman himself was not permitted to reside. When it leaked out and the outcome became clear, Newman wrote to Ullathorne with regret and withdrew from the mission. The plan was over. Accepting his decision, Ullathorne replied with sadness that he had been 'shamefully misrepresented at Rome, and that by countrymen of our own' (*L.D.* xxiii, p. 312, n.2). He was the victim of deceit.

Other controversies followed, notably with Pusey and through the debates that arose around the definition of Papal infallibility. Once more, he clashed with Manning, who had adopted an extreme ultramontane line. Nevertheless, amid the stress of controversy, there was also a triumph. In 1870 Newman managed at last to publish his *Essay in Aid of a Grammar of Assent*.

(v)

Those who know only one thing about Newman, that he made a distinction between real and notional assent, will find that distinction explained here: in general, notional assents are intellectual and abstract and do not affect our conduct, while real assent is concerned with what is concrete and stirs us to action (see *G.A.* pp. 89–91 [63–4]). Besides that, this book is unique among

Newman's works as the only one that was not occasional, in the sense of being triggered by a particular occasion or need; it was prompted rather by his lifelong desire to respond to a specific pastoral concern, to show that religious faith is rational, that it is reasonable to believe. He had expressed sharply the objection he wanted to refute in an exploratory paper in 1860:

> The great mass of Catholics know nothing of argument; how then is their faith rational? The peasant believes 'what he is told,' and if his priest told him the Holy Ghost was incarnate, he would have faith in that heresy. Catholics are forbidden to reconsider the truth of their faith.[4]

That was the problem he wanted to tackle, but the *Grammar*, for all its elegance, is not immediately easy to understand. Fortunately for us, however, Newman had a conversation with his friend and fellow Oratorian, Edward Caswall, seven years later, in 1877, and Caswall made a note of what he had told him on the fly-leaf of his copy. 'Object of the book twofold,' Caswall wrote. 'In the first part shows that you can believe what you cannot understand. In the second part that you can believe what you cannot absolutely prove.'[5] But even this note needs to be explained.

When Newman observed that you can believe what you cannot understand, he was not discounting understanding as superfluous; he meant rather that belief does not depend upon understanding. There is a distinction between them. What we may come to understand through the cool processes of abstract reasoning may indeed convince us, but without moving us to believe. Belief is a different state of mind. It is personal. When we believe, he declared, 'Persons influence us, voices melt us, looks subdue us, deeds inflame us'. We do not make sacrifices for abstractions: 'no man will be a martyr for a conclusion'; but many people give their

---

4 Hugo M. de Achaval and J. Derek Holmes (eds.), *The Theological Papers of John Henry Newman on Faith and Certainty*, (Oxford, 1976), p. 81.
5 See C. S. Dessain, *John Henry Newman*, (London, 1966; Oxford, 1980), p. 148. See also *G.A.*, pp. 495–6 [318–19].

lives for what they believe: they will 'live and die upon a dogma' (*G.A.* p. 93 [66]).

And as belief does not depend upon understanding, neither does it depend upon absolute proof. This was the second position Newman wished to establish. He wanted to show that the kind of proof that undergirds belief is not absolute according to some strict, formal demonstration, but is often made up of an accumulation or convergence of probabilities. His clearest image was not used in the *Grammar*, but appeared in a letter to one of his regular correspondents, Canon John Walker, on 6 July 1864. He likened the certitude supplied by absolute proof to an iron rod and the certitude that supports belief to 'a *cable* which is made up of a number of separate threads, each feeble', yet which, when woven together, are unbreakable (*L.D.* xxi, p. 146). I suspect that many people can recognise what he meant and agree. An obvious example for me, as rector of a seminary, occurs whenever I have to recommend someone for ordination. Have I absolute proof that the person is suitable? Of course not; I could be mistaken. But when over a significant period of time I find a pattern emerging of fidelity to prayer, intellectual competence, and pastoral commitment, all well integrated within a mature human personality, I feel able with confidence to make my recommendation. None of these elements – spiritual, intellectual, pastoral and human – taken singly, can ensure fitness for ordination, but together they combine to create certainty. And we discover that certainty by using what Newman called in the *Grammar* our illative sense, which he described as 'a grand word for a common thing' (*L.D.* xxiv, p. 375).

Illation is reasoning. The illative sense, therefore, refers to the human capacity for reasoning, our gift for assessing evidence and, Newman claimed, doing so accurately. Inadequate evidence, of course, will mislead us, but, given the evidence, as Newman had stated many years before, we commonly reason well (see *U.S.* p. 211). This confidence in the human condition was fundamental for him. When using our illative sense, we weigh the evidence, discern the patterns in the converging probabilities, and come to certitude. Moreover, for him the process was always intensely personal. As we noticed earlier, towards the end of the *Grammar* he declared, 'I say plainly I do not want to be converted by a smart syllogism; if I am asked to convert others by it, I say plainly I do not care to overcome their reason without touching their hearts' (*G.A.* p. 425 [273]).[6]

A Grammar of Assent was perhaps his crowning literary achievement. And then in 1879 there came a great surprise.

(vi)

Pope Leo XIII, who had succeeded Pius IX the previous year, planned to create new cardinals and among them, he hoped, would be Newman. It was a gracious gesture, but even so there was drama. Cardinals who were not diocesan bishops usually resided in Rome. When Newman was approached and told of the Pope's wish, he was deeply grateful for the honour that would be done him and wanted to accept, but for him to leave Birmingham at his age – he was 78 – was, he felt, impossible. All the same, he did not wish even to seem to be bargaining, putting terms on his acceptance to the Pope. He discussed his dilemma with Ullathorne who had brought him the news. Ullathorne advised him to write a letter to him, which Newman did, expressing his gratitude to the Pope and also his desire to remain in his 'much loved Oratory' (*L.D.* xxix, p. 19). Ullathorne then added a letter of his own to accompany Newman's, explaining clearly Newman's wish to accept, but his reluctance to leave Birmingham, which, he added, he was sure was never 'the Holy Father's intention' (*L.D.* xxix, p. 20). He then sent these two letters to Cardinal Manning who was due to leave for Rome and deliver them. But Manning forwarded only Newman's letter without Ullathorne's explanation, so that the desire he expressed to remain in Birmingham seemed like a refusal of the honour. He also let slip the news that Newman had refused. When that became known, there was an outcry. All

6 See above, p. 7.

kinds of people protested. And Newman's answer to inquirers who wanted to know the reason for his refusal, was plain: he could not refuse an offer which he had yet to receive; no formal invitation had been made. Manning, realising his blunder, went quickly to the Pope to put the matter right. Then the formal news of Newman's elevation was sent to Birmingham and he received his Cardinal's hat in Rome on 15 May 1879. The cloud, as he said, had been lifted from him for ever. He lived for a further eleven years, dying in 1890. He was 89.

(vii)

Newman's long life was obviously far fuller and more complex than this account can convey. His personality and ideas and the interpretation to be placed on events have led to a whole industry of Newman studies and scholarship. His genius is original and far-sighted, constantly breaking new ground. There are those whose admiration for Newman makes them believe he could do no wrong. Admiring Newman, as I do, and conscious of my debt to him, nevertheless that is not the attitude that I feel needs to be adopted here. There can always be alternative views. Newman does not win over everyone. Some find him personally too sensitive, or too ruthless in argument, or too determined always to be right. Let it be so.

All this account has tried to do is describe the path he pursued throughout his life, showing that he tried to follow it consistently and honestly. First, he was led from evangelicalism through rationalism to Anglicanism and then on to Catholicism; after that, once a Catholic, holding to the same path, he endured trials and humiliation, until unexpectedly the Pope honoured him as a Cardinal. At his death, as he declared, according to the epitaph he himself had composed, he passed out of the shadows and images into the truth: *ex umbris et imaginibus in veritatem*. That had been his desired destination all along.

3

A Mind Alive

(i)

However difficult it may be to chart the course of Newman's long and involved life, it is still more demanding to capture the character of his mind. One reason for that is something personal, something about him. It was identified neatly by Nicholas Lash when he drew attention to 'that very *closeness* of speech to speaker, of text to thinker, which is the hallmark of his genius'. Sometimes people have written about Newman's theological method and even done it rather well. Nevertheless, the theories they parade can seem stiff and alien, because, as Lash has explained, 'it is *Newman* who makes the difference to those touched by his spell, far more than his arguments or ideas considered in abstraction'.[1] While mapping the mind, we must never forget the man.

The man was always more interested in reality than theory. He was concerned with what actually happened. His sympathies lay instinctively with a process of reasoning which was direct and immediate. So in 1870, in his *Grammar of Assent*, he declared: 'I say, then, that our most natural mode of reasoning is, not from propositions to propositions, but from things to things, from concrete to concrete, from wholes to wholes' (*G.A.* p. 330 [213–14]). That was his style and we notice at once the way this approach is naturally in tune with the priority he gave to pastoral care throughout his life.[2] There will be other examples.

Besides that, when reading Newman, we may also become

---

1 Nicholas Lash, 'Tides and Twilight: Newman since Vatican II', in Ian Ker and Alan G. Hill (eds.), *Newman after a Hundred Years*, (Oxford, 1990), pp. 451–2.
2 See above, pp. 6–7.

aware of certain preoccupations which appear time after time. There are themes which give unity to his life and way of thinking. First, there was his devotion to the cause of revealed religion. Towards the end of his life, in 1877, he was to state, 'Revelation is the initial and essential idea of Christianity' (*V.M.* i, p. xlvii [29]). Stephen Dessain believed this cause was the fundamental interest of his life.[3] Next, there was his search for the Church, which we have considered already. What has been revealed, be it ever so pregnant with meaning, is void unless received. Faith receives the revelation, but faith is never disembodied. To be more precise, it is the Church, as the community of faith, that receives and seeks to live the revelation. Church and revelation are linked inseparably.

Revelation, of course, is made known in a particularly privileged way through Sacred Scripture, but it is found there, as Newman used to say, unsystematically (see *Ari.* p. 147). Consequently later, notably under the pressure of controversy, what had been received in that way needed to be given sharper focus. And so his third preoccupation was with dogma, the interpreting and distilling of what had been revealed. 'From the age of fifteen,' he remarked in his *Apologia*, 'dogma has been the fundamental principle of my religion' (*Apo.* p. 49 [54]). And what has been revealed, and received by the Church, and articulated as dogma, was meant also to be communicated. And so the fourth key preoccupation of Newman's life was with education, the need to provide people with a deeper understanding of their faith so that they might be better able to give an account of it. In his Journal in January 1863, when at such a low point in his life, he recorded that 'from first to last, education, in this large sense of the word, has been my line' (*A.W.* p. 259).

To note these four themes – revelation, the Church, dogma, and education – and the relationship between them must not, however, mislead anyone into shaping a theory of Newman's thought in their terms. They are noteworthy simply because they recur in his writing like refrains.

3 See Dessain, *John Henry Newman*, p. xii.

Nevertheless, the question remains. How can we capture the character of Newman's mind, the tenor of his thinking? How is it best to proceed? An occasion late in his life has become famous. It may be helpful to start there.

(ii)

On 12 May 1879 Newman was waiting with his friends and others who were in attendance at the Palazzo della Pigna in Rome. The misunderstanding surrounding his acceptance of the invitation to become a cardinal had been resolved. And then at 11 o'clock Cardinal Lorenzo Nina, the Secretary of State, arrived from the Vatican, bringing a brief letter, a *biglietto*, from Pope Leo XIII to inform Newman that he had that morning been made a cardinal. Newman thanked him and then made a speech which has become famous. In it he declared: 'I rejoice to say, to one great mischief I have from the first opposed myself. For thirty, forty, fifty years I have resisted to the best of my powers the spirit of Liberalism in religion.' Now, liberalism is an elusive concept. For some it is admirable because it breathes a spirit of tolerance, a lack of coercion, while for others it does harm because it is vague and ill-defined, an invitation to relativism. Newman himself was happy to praise its virtues such as justice and truthfulness; he does so later in this very speech; but here more specifically he was concerned with liberalism in religion and his view seems clear. He went on:

> Liberalism in religion is the doctrine that there is no positive truth in religion, but that one creed is as good as another ... It is inconsistent with any recognition of any religion, as *true*. It teaches that all are to be tolerated, for all are matters of opinion. Revealed religion is not a truth, but a sentiment and a taste; not an objective fact, not miraculous; and it is the right of each individual to make it say just what strikes his fancy.[4]

4 See Wilfrid Ward, *The Life of John Henry Cardinal Newman* ii, (London, 1912), p. 460.

These words have sometimes led to the claim that Newman was simply 'against the liberals'. But the truth is more subtle and more interesting. He was responding to circumstances. That does not mean he was merely being subjective himself; rather, he was reacting to the situation confronting him.

As an Anglican, championing dogma, Newman opposed those who had come to regard creeds, in his words, as 'fetters on souls' (*P.S.* ii, p. 261), and dismissed the great controversies about the Trinity and the Christ which had racked the Church in the early centuries as 'the strict and technical niceties of doctrine' (*P.S.* ii, pp. 166–7). That attitude appalled him. Expressed in those terms, it may seem to us obscure and theoretical. For Newman, however, it was immediate and exemplified in particular by the views of Renn Dickson Hampden.

Newman and Hampden

Hampden was the Principal of St Mary Hall, one of the lesser Oxford halls, who was appointed Regius Professor of Divinity at Oxford in 1836. He has been described as 'by nature a scholar; a learned man of no charisma and little charm'.[5] His appointment, however, was controversial on both political and theological grounds. There were those who rejoiced at the opportunity it gave them to embarrass Lord Melbourne's government: charges against Hampden's orthodoxy made it possible to present his preferment as a Whig attack on the faith of the Church. Others resented his selection because he favoured the admission of dissenters to the University and by doing so seemed to threaten that bastion of Anglican orthodoxy. And a few, more particularly Newman and his friends, were convinced that his writings were heretical and that he was, therefore, unfit for the post in any case. Scholars are still divided over the dispute. It is not possible or necessary to settle the issues here. David Newsome's words seem characteristically well-judged. 'In retrospect,' he has observed, 'it is difficult to resist

---

5 Newsome, *The Convert Cardinals*, pp. 94–102; quotation at p. 95.

the conclusion that everyone involved in these proceedings behaved rather badly.'[6] Our concerns are more specific.

What had roused Newman was the distinction Hampden made between the divine facts, as he called them, which are revealed in the Scriptures, and everything else. Everything else, even the Creeds proclaimed by Councils like Nicaea and Chalcedon, was, he affirmed, merely human speculation. In his pamphlet in support of dissenters being admitted to Oxford, a pamphlet which includes much good sense, he used as an example what he called 'the extreme case of the Unitarians'. Even they, he declared, had received both the Old and New Testaments and, by doing so, in his view, they had accepted the whole basis of revelation. What they rejected or explained away, he argued, was by virtue of that explaining not self-evident revealed fact, but part of human speculation.[7] This was the distinction which stirred Newman to protest.

When the controversy about Hampden's appointment was at its height, he sat up overnight and wrote a pamphlet, reviewing and criticising Hampden's position. It was called *Elucidations of Dr. Hampden's Theological Statements* and consisted of quotations from Hampden's writings, interspersed with comments of his own. He treated Hampden roughly, even, many would say, unjustly, but his purpose in the pamphlet was not to offer a poised critique of Hampden's thought, but rather, as he explained soon afterwards, to suggest 'bases for an examination of [his] opinions' (*L.D.* v, p. 233). And on 14 February he left a copy of the pamphlet at Hampden's door.

Hampden acknowledged it immediately and graciously. But his eye had been caught by one statement in particular. 'I am shocked', he observed, 'to find it attributed to me that I do not

---

6 *The Convert Cardinals*, p. 99. For his treatment of the whole affair, see pp. 94–102. See also Roderick Strange, 'Newman and Hampden', *Newman-Studien* XIV, (Sigmaringendorf, 1990), pp. 29–40.

7 See R. D. Hampden, *Observations on Religious Dissent*, (Oxford, 1835), pp. 19, 20.

hold the truths of the Trinity and the Incarnation as "revealed"; God forbid, I solemnly say, that ever such a thought should have crossed my mind, or have been really conveyed to any one by an inadvertence of expression on my part."[8] He demanded a retraction in the most explicit terms. Newman replied at once and his reply brings us to the heart of the issue.

He explained to Hampden that he was concerned with his writings, not his personal beliefs. He told him: 'I hope I am duly impressed by your serious protestation of your belief in the Trinity and Incarnation, and beg to remind you, I have no where expressed a doubt of it.' Then he went on: 'I have spoken of you only as an author, and, *as such*, you seem to lie open to my remark, for since you state in your pamphlet that an Unitarian holds "the *whole* revelation" *as holding* "the basis of divine facts", you surely do deny that "the truths of the Trinity and the Incarnation" are "revealed"' (*L.D.* v, pp. 235–6). In other words, Newman was arguing, if Unitarians, because they accept the Bible, are Christians, although they reject the Trinity and the Incarnation, how can these beliefs be upheld as revealed and essential to Christianity? That was his point. Hampden appealed indeed to revelation, but his understanding of revelation was so restricted that later formulations of dogma were in his view merely matters of truths of opinion. They could have no higher status. What was revealed was in the Bible and obvious, evident because beyond dispute; what had emerged later through controversy, having failed that criterion, could not claim the same status. It could only be speculation. And that was the viewpoint which Newman attacked.

For him, as we have seen, scripture was unsystematic. Had disputes over its interpretation not arisen, it alone would have been enough; in fact, he thought, that would have been the ideal. But it was not to be. Human reality is more complex. People argue. Interpretations of what had been revealed were disputed,

8 R. D. Hampden, Letter to J. H. Newman, 14 February 1836, *L.D.* v, p. 235; see J. H. Newman, *Elucidations of Dr. Hampden's Theological Statements*, (Oxford, 1836), p. 41.

but what had then been hammered out in controversy and defined in creeds and dogmas could not for that reason be regarded as mere speculation or a matter of opinion. When particular theological opinions came in due course to be canonised in creeds and dogmas, they acquired by that very fact a different, a higher status.

Newman explained his position in his final University Sermon in 1843, when he declared: 'Creeds and dogmas live in the one idea which they are designed to express, and which alone is substantive; ... the Catholic dogmas are, after all, but symbols of a Divine fact' (*U.S.* pp. 331–2). They symbolise the revealed truths they express, *live in* them. And the reference to symbols is telling, for Newman was writing within the literary tradition of Romantic poets like Coleridge and Wordsworth. As Stephen Prickett, former Regius Professor of English Literature at Glasgow University, has noted, 'Anyone who has read both literary criticism and theology in the Victorian period soon comes to realise how deeply the two are intertwined.'[9] Within that tradition symbols were not arbitrary, external tokens of what they express; 'form and content were essentially indivisible'; symbols were a part of, they shared in, the reality which they symbolised: 'It was not possible to describe the "meaning" of the *Ancient Mariner* in other terms than those of the poem.'[10] They had a kind of sacramental quality. That was the tradition within which Newman was working. Accordingly, dogma is privileged. It is not arbitrary, one possible expression of teaching among many. It has special status. It articulates what has been revealed and is wedded to it indissolubly.[11]

There is much more that could be said. It is not necessary to resolve the dispute between Newman and Hampden here. This, however, may be enough to illustrate, from Newman's Anglican years, his claim in 1879. Whatever the merits of Hampden's

9 See Stephen Prickett, *Romanticism and Religion: The Tradition of Coleridge and Wordsworth in the Victorian Church*, (Cambridge, 1976), p. 7.

10 Prickett, *Romanticism and Religion*, p. 219.

11 For a fuller account, see Roderick Strange, 'Dogma and Religious Truth', *Ampleforth Journal* lxxxiii (Summer 1978) 4–11.

standpoint, Newman saw himself as resisting the spirit of liberalism in religion, defending dogma against a view that would reduce it to human speculation, something not binding, a fancy a person might take or leave.

Newman and Ward

After Newman had become a Catholic in 1845, his theological work had much in common with the work of his Anglican period. There were sermons rich in theological content, detailed patristic studies, and the same abiding interest in the relationship between faith and reason. Nor had his commitment to dogma changed. But his circumstances had. For the Anglican Newman, as we have seen, the dogmatic principle had priority and needed to be safe-guarded, but as a Catholic, the scene was different. In the Catholic Church dogma was not at risk; rather the contrary, it was in the ascendant. And in the ascendant with it was a dogmatizing spirit, narrow, rigid, and authoritarian, aggressive, unimaginative, and hostile to alternatives. Those with that cast of mind found it hard, if not impossible, not to canonise their own opinions as definitive and condemn any alternative as unsound. If his dispute with Hampden can be said to illustrate Newman's attitude and approach during his Anglican years, then his relationship with W. G. Ward may do the same while he was a Catholic.

W. G. Ward was a gifted pure mathematician. It is perhaps significant that he could not bear applied mathematics. He delighted in pushing arguments to their logical conclusion and that approach marked his theology as well. As a young man at Oxford he had at first taken no interest in the Tractarians. Urged to hear Newman preach, he had dismissed the notion out of hand: 'Why should I go and listen to such myths?'[12] he asked. But later he went and, once he had done so, his life was changed. He became at first one of Newman's most enthusiastic followers.

12 See Wilfrid Ward, *William Ward and the Oxford Movement*, (London, 1889), p. 80.

Ward's enthusiasm led him to be received into the Catholic
Church before Newman. He became an extreme Ultramontane.
He is famous for wishing to have 'a new papal Bull every morning
with my *Times* at breakfast', although people usually fail to
recognise the paradoxical humour underlying the remark.[13] Ward
was an engaging character, blessed with a keen sense of humour. I
particularly enjoy the story of the time when he went to the
theatre in King William Street. The theatre itself had previously
been the home of the London Oratorians before they moved to
Brompton with Frederick Faber as their Superior. Faber was
another warm-hearted enthusiast who had been a disciple of
Newman's and also tended to extremism. He and Newman were
to clash bitterly. Faber was Ward's spiritual director. On this
occasion, however, sitting in the theatre between acts Ward was
struck by two thoughts. 'The first', he later admitted to Faber,
'was, Last time I was in this building I heard Faber preach. The
second was, How much more I am enjoying myself tonight than I
did the last time I was here.'[14]

Ward always retained an affection for Newman in spite of their
differences. Years later he was to tell him that those differences
made him feel 'a kind of intellectual orphan'.[15] Newman for his
part remained fond of Ward; nevertheless he became exasperated
by Ward's dogmatizing spirit, the way he exaggerated devotion to
Mary and advocated an extreme view of papal authority. We shall
come across examples later.

He also became weary of Ward's confidence in his own opinions, his tendency to regard even minor differences as matters of
great moment. He described their relationship adroitly in a letter
in 1862. Ward had asked if he could pay him a visit and Newman
replied, welcoming him. But he then sketched how he foresaw the
pattern of their conversation.

---

13 See Wilfrid Ward, *William George Ward and the Catholic Revival*, (London,
    1893), p. 14.
14 See Ward, *William Ward and the Catholic Revival*, pp. 65–6.
15 See Ward, *William Ward and the Oxford Movement*, p. 81.

If things are to go as they have gone, I should anticipate our conversation would have this result: viz, you would begin by stating that I hold something very different from, or the reverse of, what I really hold. I should undeceive you, and you would confess that you were mistaken. Then we should branch off to some independent subject of theology, and you would be pleased to find that I agreed with you, when others did not. You would leave – and then, in a few weeks, you would write me word, that it pained you bitterly to think that we were diverging from each other in theological opinion more and more. If I then wrote to inquire what you could mean, you would answer that you really could not at the moment recollect the grounds on which you had been led to say so; but you would not withdraw it.

Thus I have to endure, in spite of your real affection for me, a never-dying misgiving on your part that I am in some substantial matter at variance with you – while I for my part sincerely think that on *no* subject is there any substantial difference between us, as far as theology is concerned (*L.D.* xx, p. 191).

That final phrase, 'as far as theology is concerned', is revealing because it pointed to a situation which Ward's position and cast of mind found it hard to allow: the legitimate co-existence of differing points of view. He never learnt the lesson which Newman had tried to teach him earlier, 'to bear and forbear' (*L.D.* xvi, p. 486). That was Newman's standpoint, his priority as a Catholic, where dogma was secure, but theology under threat. He always prized dogma, but as a Catholic he championed freedom in theology as well, because he was aware of the threat posed by dogmatic fundamentalism.

(iii)

Newman's appreciation of theology was expressed most precisely in 1877, when he called it 'the fundamental and regulating

principle of the whole Church system' (*V.M.* i, p. xlvii [29]). He
was preparing his *Lectures on the Prophetical Office* for inclusion in
the uniform edition of his works. He did not wish to alter the text
which he had prepared forty years earlier; his policy was, *litera
scripta manent*; but the changes in his views from the time when he
had been writing this book and at the peak of his influence as an
Anglican, to this time, when he had been a Catholic for more than
thirty years, were so great that it called for something more than
explanatory footnotes. He decided, therefore, to write a special
preface for this new edition. It has become famous. In it he
reflected not only on the prophetical office of the original title, but
on the priestly and kingly offices as well; and indeed he considered
their relationships to one another. It was while discussing these
three offices that he spoke of theology as the fundamental and
regulating principle. He called it that because he regarded it as
'commensurate with Revelation', and he called revelation 'the
initial and essential idea of Christianity'. We are back to the first of
those four preoccupations to which I referred at the beginning of
this chapter, his devotion to revealed religion. And from revelation
and its theology, he went on to argue, priesthood and kingship
flow (see *V.M.* i, p. xlvii [29]). All the same, nowadays the
attention given to the offices may seem rather static. Some time
later, Baron Friedrich von Hügel took up the idea in more
dynamic terms.

Von Hügel did not concentrate on the offices so much as the
adjectives which go with them: kings lead institutions, and so are
concerned with what is institutional; prophets teach, and so are
concerned with what is intellectual; and priests, celebrating the
mysteries, should be devoted to the mystical.[16] And so we shift
from the titles, king, prophet and priest, to the qualities they
imply, the institutional, the intellectual and the mystical. By doing

---

16 See Friedrich von Hügel, *The Mystical Element of Religion as Studied in Saint
Catherine of Genoa and her Friends*, (London, 1923), i, pp. 50–5. The prompt
for much of what follows comes from Michael Paul Gallagher SJ, 'Faith
Development of Seminarians', *Seminary Journal* 4/3 (Winter 1998) 22–33.

so, we also come to recognise more readily the virtues which go with those qualities: what is institutional demands loyalty, what is intellectual prompts questioning, while what is mystical invites contemplation. And these qualities and their virtues are not static. They grow, develop, mature. And while they need to be inter-woven as constant elements in our lives, each has a time when it seems to command priority.

Loyalty is, first of all, a characteristic of children. What we first encounter, our earliest experiences, we take to be normal at the start and guard loyally. Later, as adolescents, we discover that life is not so simple and we find ourselves stirred to ask a range of questions. Then, as we move into maturity, the perspective changes again: we are led on to gaze, to contemplate. It is not a matter of moving distinctly and cleanly from one phase to the next. They are not independent compartments. Each quality is to be valued and maintained and they need to be integrated. When those who are loyal confront questions, they do not, therefore, become disloyal; rather their loyalty is refined. And, as they move into contemplation, they may still wrestle with questions, but the struggle has changed character, become less anxious, more tranquil.

What makes this approach particularly significant here, how-ever, is the part played by questioning – in this context, by theology. Newman called it fundamental and regulating and it is possible to see why. He was not making what is rational supreme, but recognising it instead as the hinge for our development. Understanding, intellectual activity, challenges our initial loyalties, checks our prejudices, and frees us from our rigid, preconceived ideas. And then, as we explore it and discover its limitations, we find ourselves being ushered into a place beyond intellectual achievement alone, where we gaze, contemplate, and plumb still greater depths. Theology is the regulating hinge. It matures our loyalty and launches us into contemplation.

Newman's commitment to dogma was never obscurantist, a refusal to face questioning. He valued theology; he regarded its role as indispensable, as we shall see. But, returning to his speech in

1879, the question may still be raised: if, during his Catholic years, his approach to theology was sound and dogma was secure, in what sense could he be said to have been resisting religious liberalism? Yet, in fact, he had. But the target was not so much anti-dogmatic Christian believers; it was rather, what he called, 'a darkness different in kind from any that has been before it'.[17]

(iv)

That phrase comes from a sermon he preached in 1873 which is called 'The Infidelity of the Future'. Newman looked ahead and tried to describe the kind of society which he foresaw developing and in which the Catholic Church must live. Many details ring true today in the western world: the waning influence of other Christian communities; the resistance to Catholicism, particularly when its influence is felt to grow; the setbacks created by scandals; the problems which arise from shallow thinking, what we might call media culture, for, in Newman's words, 'a fool may ask a hundred questions which a wise man cannot answer'; and the genuine difficulties which there are in revealed religion in any case. But the root cause of these features he identified in a single sentence: 'Christianity has never yet had experience of a world simply irreligious.'[18] Is this prediction too bleak? Not obviously.

In western society today, as we know, personal freedom is so cherished that nothing must be allowed to threaten it; but that is what the claim of revealed religion as objectively true appears to do. Objective truth would have to take priority. In western eyes that cannot be permitted. Personal freedom must never be restrained. What is possible is in general assumed to be permissible, in relationships, in science, in medicine, in professional or political life. We test the limits like adolescents, often insensitive to a moral or ethical dimension. In any case, we ask, what is truth?

17 *Catholic Sermons of Cardinal Newman*, edited at the Birmingham Oratory, (London, 1957), p. 121.
18 *Catholic Sermons*, p. 123; see also pp. 125–31.

The concept of 'objective truth' is, of course, a difficult one. Western society may once have defended it, but the critique has kept moving, dissolving confidence in coherence, in finding meaning, and in commitment. The narrative has collapsed. Here is the fragmentation known as post-modernism. Viewpoints shatter and relationships break down. Where are we to turn? In such a landscape, confused, fragmented, uncommitted, western society argues that only the personal is secure, the subjective, the relative. It is in many respects the scene which Newman foresaw, a view of the world in which religion has no place.

Someone else who has recognised that is Pope Benedict XVI. Preaching to the College of Cardinals on 18 April 2005 at the Mass before they entered the conclave from which he himself in fact was to emerge as Pope, he used the image of the Church as a boat, tossed on the waves created by ideological currents, 'from Marxism to liberalism, even to libertinism; from collectivism to radical individualism; from atheism to a vague religious mysticism; from agnosticism to syncretism and so forth'. He was regarded at the time as excessively pessimistic, particularly when he concluded, 'We are building a dictatorship of relativism that does not recognise anything as definitive and whose ultimate goal consists solely of one's own ego and desires.'[19] His phrase, 'the dictatorship of relativism', may seem severe, and yet it can be linked to Newman's, 'a world simply irreligious'. And the connection is not necessarily a coincidence.

For Pope Benedict relativism is a threat because, when we abandon objective truth, it is not that nothing is true, but that anything can be true. And it gets worse. For where there are no criteria to safeguard truth, you do not have tolerance; you have whatever truth those in power decide it should be. Freedom divorced from truth will not be protected; it will be lost. When we abandon truth, we abandon freedom as well. And so the Pope has spoken of the abandonment of objective truth as a slide into

19 See *Give Yourself to Christ: First Homilies of Pope Benedict XVI*, (London, 2005), p. 18.

totalitarianism, placing us at the mercy of the dictator. The reference to totalitarianism may seem emotive and extreme, but we should remember that Benedict has experience of what he is saying.[20]

He has addressed the issue on a number of occasions, but one which is particularly notable here was the Conference held in Rome in 1990 to mark the centenary of Newman's death. On that occasion he referred to the bond between truth and personal conscience.

As Cardinal Ratzinger, he spoke first about his own introduction to Newman's thought when he was a young seminarian shortly after the Second World War and he went on to stress at once the importance for him of Newman's teaching on conscience. Newman taught that conscience was to be cherished, he explained, as 'a way of obedience to objective truth'. And Newman's whole life bore witness to that conviction. The future Pope's earlier experience, however, had been very different. 'We had experienced', he told the Conference, 'the claim of a totalitarian party which understood itself as the fulfilment of history and which negated the conscience of the individual. One of its leaders [Hermann Goering] had said: "I have no conscience. My conscience is Adolf Hitler."'[21] Here is the slide into totalitarianism. When truth is disregarded, when there is no objective standard to which we can appeal, we do not create space for easy tolerance. Instead freedom is left defenceless, at the mercy of those in power.

The young Joseph Ratzinger experienced what Newman had at least implicitly predicted, the consequences when revealed religion is not recognised as true, as objective, but is regarded as something private from which people may select for themselves whatever they fancy.

20 See John L. Allen, Jr., *The Rise of Benedict XVI*, (New York, 2005), pp. 165–6, 174–8.

21 Joseph Ratzinger, 'Newman Belongs to the Great Teachers of the Church', in Peter Jennings (ed.), *Benedict XVI and Cardinal Newman*, (Oxford, 2005), p. 33.

(v)

There is, of course, far more to the pattern of Newman's thought than this brief account can indicate; other aspects will emerge as we proceed; but his speech in Rome in 1879 when he was made a Cardinal at least offers us a perspective. His opposition to religious liberalism and his commitment to the dogmatic principle shaped his approach throughout his life, whether he was in controversy with those indifferent to dogma in his early Anglican days or working to overcome the narrower dogmatizing spirit which he discovered later among Catholics. In both instances he was inspired by the same principle. And then there was the challenge of infidelity.

The dovetailing of his view on religious liberalism with the position adopted by Pope Benedict XVI, a position possibly influenced by Newman's own standpoint, suggests the next step we should take. In 1870 the Catholic teaching on papal infallibility was defined as a dogma. The definition delighted some and distressed others. There was controversy beforehand and debate afterwards. Newman found himself drawn into the fray. His position has often been regarded as significant, offering a wise interpretation of what was declared.

4

Infallible Authority

(i)

In 1967 Pope Paul VI made a statement that startled many people. Addressing the Secretariat for Promoting Christian Unity on 28 April that year, he declared: 'The Pope, as we well know, is undoubtedly the gravest obstacle in the path of ecumenism.'[1] And Pope John Paul II was in a way echoing the same sentiment when he acknowledged that papal primacy, which should have been a service, 'sometimes manifested itself in a very different light' (*Ut Unum Sint*, no. 95). Both men were recognising the difficulty people have had understanding the nature of papal ministry. And the difficulty has not only been felt by those outside the Catholic Church; some of those within have also been critical. Father Hans Küng is the obvious example with his book, *Infallible?*, published in 1970 to coincide with the centenary of the formal definition of papal infallibility at the First Vatican Council.

Küng felt impelled to write because he believed the legacy of Pope John XXIII and the Second Vatican Council was being squandered by the way in which Paul VI was exercising the Petrine ministry. The Council's emphasis on dialogue and consultation was, he argued, being ignored in favour of the old absolutist style. He praised the Pope's good intentions, but was dismayed by his decisions about priestly celibacy and contraception, and by his tendency to accord certain Roman theological opinions a status he felt they did not deserve. So many years later it

---

1 See Thomas F. Stransky and John B. Sheerin, *Doing the Truth in Charity: Statements of Pope Paul VI, Popes John Paul I, John Paul II, and the Secretariat for Promoting Christian Unity, 1964-1980*, (New York, 1982), p. 273.

makes no sense to try to settle those specific issues here. They still arouse debate, but the scene Küng described has shifted. The tension now is seen rather to lie between restoration and renewal. All the same, Küng's fundamental concern remains significant. 'Even when the Church's claim to infallibility is not explicit,' he remarked, 'it is always subliminally present.'[2] What makes it noteworthy is the way it dovetails with concerns expressed a hundred years earlier.

During the preparations for the First Vatican Council, when the desire developed for papal infallibility to be defined formally as a dogma of the Church, some people opposed it. They did not do so in general because they denied the teaching, but because they feared too extravagant a definition. It was a difficult time.

Among the bishops who favoured the definition, however, and championed it, one of the most prominent was Henry Manning, the Archbishop of Westminster. His relationship with Newman had once been warm, but had become much cooler. And after the Council Manning wrote a long pastoral letter to the priests of his diocese, to introduce and explain what had been defined. In it he included within the infallible authority of the Pope as part of 'the whole revealed order of salvation', such matters as 'Things which pertain to faith', 'Things pertaining to piety', 'Things of religion', 'Things of faith speculative and practical', and 'Controversies of religion'.[3] The very looseness of language was liable to arouse suspicion. Where were the limits? Manning's approach seemed to be sowing the seeds of what has come to be called 'creeping infallibility', an exercise of infallible authority that seems at first to grow so gradually it is hardly noticed, but then could run out of control. What delighted him made others anxious. And those who were anxious often turned to Newman.

Some years later, when he was drawn into the controversy more

2 Hans Küng, *Infallible?*, (London, 1971), p. 23.
3 See H. E. Manning, *The Vatican Council and its Definitions: a pastoral letter to the Clergy*, (London, 1870), pp. 65–6; reprinted in H. E. Manning, *Petri Privilegium*, (London, 1871).

publicly, Newman was to observe that the upset felt by many had often been caused by Catholics themselves. He was critical of extreme enthusiasts. For years, he wrote, there have been those who 'have conducted themselves as if no responsibility attached to wild words and overbearing deeds; who have stated truths in the most paradoxical form, and stretched principles till they were close upon snapping; and who at length, having done their best to set the house on fire, leave to others the task of putting out the flame' (*Diff.* ii, pp. 176–7). By that time he had been fire-fighting for years.

(ii)

As we have seen, the Anglican Newman had regarded infallibility, if it existed at all, as a characteristic of the undivided Church. Since, as he then believed, the Church Catholic had split into several branches, Roman, Eastern, and Anglican, it had forfeited that gift. He put it starkly: '. . . since the Church is now not one, it is not infallible; . . . the full prophetical idea is not now fulfilled' (*V.M.* i, p. 201 [228]). He preferred to speak of indefectibility, the confidence that the Church would not fail.

As he moved towards the Catholic Church, however, he rejected this branch theory of the Church. Moreover, as he reflected more deeply on the nature of Christianity as revelation and indeed as a revelation whose depths become known gradually through development, so he became convinced of the presence in the Church of infallibility as that necessary gift which is able to recognise and guarantee the truth of the teaching that emerged. He acknowledged the distinction between a revelation and its guarantee as true; the one did not inevitably imply the other: a revelation did not have to be guaranteed. All the same, he argued that Christianity is different because it comes precisely as a reve-lation, 'as a whole, objectively, and with a profession of infall-ibility' (see *Dev.* pp. 79–80).

Arguments about infallibility will continue. Newman set out his own understanding in various places, notably in his *Essay on*

Development and his *Apologia*. The point to recognise here is that he was himself convinced of it independently of the teaching of the First Vatican Council. It was not something about which he had doubts, but felt forced to accept once the Pope in Council had proclaimed the definition. Nonetheless, he had not been a supporter of the definition as such. On 20 September 1869 he made a rough note and asked himself a question: 'Why is it, if I believe the Pope's Infallibility I do not wish it defined?' And he replied, 'I answer, because it can't be so defined as not to raise more questions than it solves' (*L.D.* xxiv, p. 334, n.2). It was the possible terms of the definition that worried him.

During the Council, as he became aware of the vigour with which those who favoured the definition were pursuing their objective, his anxiety grew and he became indignant. On 28 January 1870 he wrote a private letter to his own bishop, William Ullathorne, which came to be known. In it he criticised the desire to define papal infallibility as unnecessary, because people in practice believed it in any case; a definition, he wrote, would be 'thunder in the clear sky, and we are told to prepare for something we know not what to try our faith we know not how'. He also criticised the move as unhistorical. 'When has definition of doctrine de fide been a luxury of devotion,' he asked, 'and not a stern painful necessity?' And he denounced the 'aggressive insolent faction . . . [who] "make the heart of the just to mourn, whom the Lord hath not made sorrowful"' (*L.D.* xxv, pp. 18–19). It was not an isolated protest.

On 21 August in the same year he wrote to his friend, Ambrose St John, and referred to 'the tyrant majority'. He advised a policy of perfect quiet, in case it 'should do something more' (*L.D.* xxv, p. 192). But perhaps his most withering protest came in his letter to Margaret Wilson, a convert to Catholicism, who felt she may have been received into the Church too soon. She was worried about the definition and unsettled by rumours of priests who would not give the sacraments to people who could not accept the new dogma. Newman sent her a letter on 20 October and declared: 'I think there are some Bishops and Priests, who act as if they did not care whether souls were lost or not – and only wish to save souls on their own measure' (*L.D.* xxv, p. 216). Such an indictment of certain members of the clergy as careless and selfishly callous in the way they were exercising their pastoral responsibilities could scarcely be more damning. It touched him profoundly. Some days later, he told another friend, David Moriarty, who was the Bishop of Kerry, that such behaviour 'so pierces my heart, I do not know what to do – and I rise in indignation against such cruelty' (*L.D.* xxv, p. 223).

What he did, in fact, was to develop a strategy for those who wrote to him in distress. He pleaded with them not to confuse the doctrine that had been defined with the manner in which it was passed. A letter to Catherine Froude, a longstanding friend, early in 1871 is typical of his approach. He tried to reassure her: 'As little as possible was passed at the Council – nothing about the Pope which I have not myself always held – but it is impossible to deny that it was done with an imperiousness and overbearing wilfulness, which has been a great scandal' (*L.D.* xxv, p. 262). Such remarks were a common feature of his letters at that time (See *L.D.* xxv, pp. 224, 277–8; *L.D.* xxvi, p. 11).

And he consoled those who were troubled further by reminding them of the lesson of history. To one he wrote: 'if you look into history, you find Popes continually completing the acts of their predecessors, and Councils too – sometimes only half the truth is brought out at one time – I doubt not a coming Pope, or a coming Council, will so explain and guard what has now been passed by [the] late Council, as to clear up all that troubles us now' (*L.D.* xxv, p. 322). And another he told: 'Let us be patient, let us have faith, and a new pope, and a re-assembled Council may trim the boat' (*L.D.* xxv, p. 310).

These letters in particular give a sense of the fretful atmosphere at the time and how Newman handled the controversy that swirled around the defining of papal infallibility. In brief, he was against the definition for two principal reasons. First of all, he believed it to be unnecessary. Formerly definitions had been made to combat particular heresies. But that reason did not hold good in the present instance, and, he observed, 'It is dangerous to go beyond the rule of tradition in such a matter' (*L.D.* xxiv, p. 377). Here he was anticipating the remarks he was to make even more trenchantly to his bishop in January 1870, when he spoke of the definition as 'thunder in a clear sky' and 'a luxury of devotion, and not a stern painful necessity' (*L.D.* xxv, pp. 18–19). Then connected with this first reason was the second: because the definition was unnecessary it unsettled people's minds. He was aware of the distress which was being caused by the letters he received from those who asked for his advice. The definition made the defence of Catholicism more difficult (see *L.D.* xxvi, p. 139).

Newman's reaction to the definition is, therefore, quite plain: while he had no difficulty in accepting it and as a Catholic at least had always held it, he was scandalised by the behaviour of those who had championed it, and considered the definition itself both unnecessary and pastorally disadvantageous.[4] There remains the further question of what he understood the gift of infallibility to mean.

(iii)

In 1874, when William Gladstone lost the General Election, he attributed his misfortune in part to the influence that he felt the Pope had exercised in Ireland, an influence that undermined his position. He was mistaken, but that conviction led him to attack the decrees of the Vatican Council. He produced a popular pamphlet in which he claimed that on account of those decrees Roman Catholics had forfeited their moral and mental freedom and placed their civil loyalty and duty under the Pope. As citizens they were no longer to be trusted. Newman was the person to whom many people turned for an answer to those charges.

He struggled for a while before deciding how to reply, but

---

4 For a fuller account of Newman's view, see C. S. Dessain, 'Infallibility: What Newman taught in Manning's Church', in M. D. Goulder (ed.), *Infallibility in the Church*, (London, 1968), pp. 59–80.

eventually he wrote at some speed his *Letter to the Duke of Norfolk*. He struggled partly because he knew and admired Gladstone, although he believed him to be wrong in this instance; however, he also struggled because he wanted his response to offer an alternative view to the exaggerated claims that people like W. G. Ward and those who agreed with him, not to mention Archbishop Manning, were inclined to make. The situation was delicate. He asserted, however, that some Catholics could largely blame themselves for alienating Gladstone, and this was the occasion when he described the language and behaviour of these enthusiasts as often irresponsible, setting the house on fire and leaving to others 'the task of putting out the flame' (*Diff.* ii, pp. 176–7).

Newman's *Letter to the Duke of Norfolk*, answering Gladstone's charges, draws material together and covers a range of particular subjects, such as the nature of the Church, the Papacy, conscience, the Syllabus of Errors, and issues arising from the Vatican Council itself and inevitably it is shaped by the controversy. For our purposes, however, the core of his position emerges more precisely from his correspondence, the letters he wrote to particular individuals, responding to their concerns and anxieties and answering their questions. Reviewing those letters, four points arise regularly, points which are as essential for us today as they were in the years immediately following the First Vatican Council. In fact when I am being questioned about infallibility, these are the issues to which almost always I find myself returning.[5]

(iv)

First of all, Newman used to insist that infallibility is an external gift. It is not some sort of inherent quality of the Pope's mind, influencing every judgment he makes. In a brief, dense letter on 17 September 1872 to one correspondent who may have been the Anglo-Catholic controversialist, R. F. Littledale, he wrote:

---

5 Without mentioning him by name, Newman's influence helped guide my account of infallibility in *The Catholic Faith*, pp. 76–80.

'Infallibility is not a *habit* in the Pope, or a state of mind – ' It was, he stressed, an external, not an internal, aid. He repeated that the Pope 'has no habit of infallibility in his intellect, such that his *acts cannot but* proceed from it, *must* be infallible *because* he is infallible, *imply*, *involve*, an infallible judgment'. It is not as though the Pope cannot avoid being infallible. When then does he act infallibly? 'He is infallible,' Newman explained, '*pro re nata* [according to the circumstances], *when* he speaks ex cathedra – not except at particular times and on grave questions.' And Newman held this view because he recognised that the Pope's infallibility did not belong to him as a gift to a private person, but was 'that infallibility which the Church has'. The Pope is not infallible habitually, but as the Church is infallible; he exercises his gift only when he speaks *ex cathedra* (*L.D.* xxvi, p. 171).

What does that expression, *ex cathedra*, mean? It roots the Pope's teaching in the life of the Church. That was the second point which Newman always wished to make plain. The *cathedra*, of course, is the bishop's chair, the place from which symbolically he gives his most solemn teaching.

On 1 November 1870 Newman wrote to Lady Catherine Simeon who had become a Catholic nine years earlier and was typical of those who were distressed and confused by the new definition. He began as usual by comforting her and pointing out how limited the definition had been. Then he continued: 'The whole body of theologians ... have always held, that what the Pope said ex cathedra, was true, *when* the Bishops had received it – what has been passed, is to the effect that what he determines ex cathedra is true *independently* of the reception by the Bishops – ' In other words, he was pointing out what was novel in the Council's Decree: when the Pope acts infallibly, he does not need the consent of the bishops, he can act on his own. And then he went on, 'but nothing has been passed as to *what is meant* by "ex cathedra" – and this falls back to the Bishops and the Church to determine quite as much as before' (*L.D.* xxv, p. 224). Here he was recognising that, even when acting alone, the Pope's infallibility was not something merely private; it was still the infallibility of the Church, for that was what *ex cathedra* implied. Papal infallibility is never exercised in isolation. When the Pope acts infallibly, he necessarily acts in relation to the Church as a whole. Already at this early stage, therefore, Newman was beginning to explore the delicate issue of the relationship between papal infallibility and the infallibility of the Church, a topic which was to become central to debates ninety years later at Vatican II.

His third point referred to the object of infallible statements and so the limits of infallibility, what it involves and what it does not. In his letter of 17 September 1872, he said it was concerned with 'grave matters' which may seem rather vague, but writing to Lady Simeon he was specific: 'the decree is limited to faith and morals' (*L.D.* xxv, p. 224). A few months later, in a letter to Catherine Froude, he declared: 'certainly the Pope is not infallible beyond the Deposit of faith originally given' (*L.D.* xxv, p. 297). And these words, of course, anticipate the teaching of Vatican II that the infallibility with which the Church is endowed and which the Pope enjoys by virtue of his office, 'extends as far as the deposit of divine revelation' (*Lumen Gentium*, no. 25). The first of what I have called Newman's preoccupations returns once more, revelation.

And we need to remember that revelation is much more than privileged information; it is the source of that essential self-knowledge which the Church needs in order to be itself. Individuals who lack sufficient knowledge of themselves become mentally unbalanced, like the man who once came into my room in Oxford and declared, 'I am the Pope and you are under obedience to me.' Needless to say, it was not Pope John Paul II on a private visit, but a man I knew well, who was schizophrenic and had stopped taking his medication. But what is sickness in individuals is still more disastrous for communities. If a community loses serious hold of its self-understanding, it may not only become unbalanced, it will lose its identity. It is what provokes schism. Revelation, the deposit of faith and morals, what we believe and how we should behave, supplies that essential self-knowledge for the Church so that it may be true to itself. And the gift of infallibility is at its service. It does not rove around, pronouncing on lesser matters. It protects and safeguards what has been revealed. The Church's infallibility, Newman told another correspondent, Alfred Plummer, on 3 April 1871, 'means she can never be *permitted* to *go wrong in the truths of revelation*'.

Then he indicated at once something else that those words imply; it is the fourth point on which he used to insist: 'This is a negative proposition – the very idea of infallibility is a negative . . . properly speaking, inspiration is positive and infallibility is negative' (*L.D.* xxv, p. 309). However, this stress upon infallibility as negative should not be interpreted as diminishing it. On the contrary, it is a healthy way of recognising that infallible definitions do not exhaust the truth they declare. What they say is not untrue, but there may still be further depths to uncover, depths which may even qualify what has presently been defined. Nevertheless the definition is a sure guide. Only the month before writing to Plummer he had told Catherine Froude, 'A Pope is not *inspired*; he has no inherent gift of divine knowledge, but when he speaks ex Cathedra, he may say little or much, but he is simply protected from saying what is untrue' (*L.D.* xxv, p. 299). Even on 'grave matters', as he told Littledale, 'the gift [of infallibility] is negative' (*L.D.* xxvi, p. 171).

Infallibility, therefore, as Newman explained it, is a gift, not a habit, at the service of what has been revealed. Being a negative gift, what it declares is not exhaustive, and its exercise, whether in Council or by the Pope *ex cathedra*, is always rooted in the life of the Church. That is its context.

(v)

This essential link to the Church's life was expressed by the Second Vatican Council as involving a responsibility laid on the Pope and bishops, when defining dogma, to 'work sedulously through the appropriate means duly to investigate . . . revelation and give it suitable expression' (*Lumen Gentium*, no. 25). Commenting on this obligation to study before defining, Bishop Christopher Butler, who was one of the Council Fathers, has observed that failure to do so would be 'a grievous sin'.[6]

The part played by study in the exercise of infallibility was also something close to Newman's heart. He emphasised the need for 'human means, research, consulting theologians etc' (*L.D.* xxvi, p. 171). He was always keen to explain the role played by the *schola theologorum*, the different theological schools. Some years before the Council he discussed it in a letter to another acquaintance, Henry Oxenham.

After describing the way the different schools of Alexandria, Antioch and Rome had worked on one another in the early Church and lamenting the effective demise of all but the Roman school, he went on to describe the *schola* as not only defending, articulating and protecting dogma, but as a teaching which is wider and fuller than apostolic dogma. It has a larger scope. He spoke of it as studying the opinion of the Church and identified it as 'the arena on which questions of development and change are argued out', so that, if changes are to come, it prepares the way and prevents surprise and scandal. Without the *schola*, he observed, 'the dogma of the Church would be the raw flesh without skin' (*L.D.* xxii, p. 99). And in his *Letter to the Duke of Norfolk*, responding to Gladstone, he stated: 'None but the *Schola Theologorum* is competent to determine the force of Papal and Synodal utterances, and the exact interpretation of them is a work of time' (*Diff.* ii, p. 176).

The strength of these statements, of course, may give rise to another question. Isy Froude, Catherine's daughter, wrote to Newman and asked it. She wondered whether, 'If the Schola Theologorum decides the meaning of a Pope or a Council's words, the Schola is infallible, not *they* or *he*'. Newman's answer called attention to the need for words to be interpreted, however clear they might appear to be. 'God is love', for example, cannot be made grounds for concluding that '*Therefore* there is no future punishment for bad men'. 'Some power then is needed', he told her, 'to determine the general sense of authoritative words – to

---

6 Christopher Butler, *The Theology of Vatican II*, (London, 1981), pp. 93–4.

determine their direction, drift, limits, and comprehension, to hinder gross perversions.' He described this power as 'virtually the *passive infallibility* of the whole body of the Catholic people', in contrast to the 'active infallibility' of the Pope and bishops. The passive and the active form an alliance. 'The body of the faithful never can misunderstand what the Church determines by the gift of its active infallibility.' We are back to the words of St Augustine which had had so profound an influence upon him, 'Securus judicat orbis terrarum' – the universal Church is in its judgments secure of truth (*L.D.* xxvii, pp. 337–8).

It is evident too that Newman did not regard this passive infallibility as something merely receptive, which would make it scarcely distinguishable from blind obedience. In August 1870 he wrote to another friend, Frederick Rymer, who was President of St Edmund's College, Ware, the seminary for the Westminster Diocese. He quoted St Augustine's words again, and told him that he regarded 'the general acceptance, judgment of Christendom' as 'the ultimate guarantee of revealed truth' (*L.D.* xxv, p. 172). And in his letter to Isy Froude he made it plain that what is infallible passively none the less acts. He was referring particularly to the *schola*. It acts, he affirmed, by correcting the popular mis-understandings and narrow views of teaching which may arise from active infallibility; also, because it is concerned essentially with investigating and debating issues, it keeps clear the distinction between theological truth and theological opinion. It is, Newman affirmed, 'the antagonist of dogmatism'. And while differences between theologians maintain liberty of thought, their unanimity 'is the safeguard of the infallible decisions of the Church and the champion of faith' (*L.D.* xxvii, pp. 337–8).

This teaching of Newman's on the role of the laity and of theologians in determining the understanding of revealed truth was a further anticipation of the view adopted by the Second Vatican Council. There it was stated: 'The universal body of the faithful who have received the anointing of the holy one, cannot be mistaken in belief. It displays this particular quality through a supernatural sense of the faith in the whole people when "from the

bishops to the last of the faithful laity", it expresses the consent of
all in matters of faith and morals' (*Lumen Gentium*, no. 12).

(vi)

To express the matter briefly, therefore, the gift of infallibility
according to Newman is an external, not an internal, aid, negative
in character and employed only in judgments which, while they
deal with revealed truth, are none the less established by human
means. To some this view may appear so restricted as to empty the
Church's teaching on infallibility of all meaning whatsoever. But
that would be a mistake. On 3 April 1871 Newman wrote to
Alfred Plummer. After pointing out that the Church teaches by
human means, although assisted by grace like any other inquirer,
he explained: 'she has *in kind* no promise of invincible grace,
which a Father or a divine, or an inquirer has not – but she has this
security, that, *in order* to fulfil her office, her *out come* is always true
in the matter of revelation' (*L.D.* xxv, p. 309). The grace is not
special, but the outcome, when it concerns revelation, is assured.

This security is no mean thing. Early in 1870, while the Council
was still in session, Newman in his *Grammar of Assent* had discussed
the distinction between infallibility and certitude. He commented
on the objection that it is not possible to believe in an infallible
Church without some infallible means of knowing the Church is
infallible. But the argument, he answered, rests on a confusion
between infallibility and certitude. We can be certain something is
true, although we sometimes make mistakes. 'For example,' he
remarked, 'I remember for certain what I did yesterday, but still
my memory is not infallible'. And shortly afterwards he observed:
'An infallible authority is certain in every particular case that may
arise; but a man who is certain in some one definite case, is not on
that account infallible' (*G.A.* pp. 224–5 [146–7]). For the Church,
the particular cases will always be limited by the revealed deposit
and the negative character of infallibility itself, but in those circumstances and according to those conditions its judgments have
the assurance of a divine promise that it will not be in error.

Such a guarantee should never be underestimated. It means that the infallible Church, when teaching revealed matters, can never so mistake the message that what it teaches would lead people directly away from God. It does not prevent the Church from being in error on less essential issues, but that is only to say that the prerogative of infallibility is confined to revealed truth; nor does it mean that its teaching is always as full and as accurate as it might be, but that is only to say that the Church is human and a pilgrim and that the gift of infallibility is negative. A merely indefectible Church, on the other hand, could presumably teach something destructive of revealed truth and detrimental to salvation for many generations, and would only be assured of returning to what is true in the end. That is not enough. Unless the Church of Christ can guarantee that what it teaches on essential matters is at the very least not false, it is nothing.

Clearly such a claim is slight and not the self-aggrandising force that those who are not Catholics sometimes fear. At the same time such a guarantee is momentous, for it safeguards the essential purity of what the Church teaches as to be believed of necessity. This minimal claim and bed-rock guarantee make up the heart of Newman's understanding of infallibility.

5

Mary, the Mother of Jesus

(i)

If the Petrine ministry is one obstacle on the path to Church unity, another is the controversy that has arisen around questions connected with Catholic teaching about Mary, the mother of Jesus. When Archbishop Michael Ramsey of Canterbury came to Rome to visit Pope Paul VI in March 1966 for their historic meeting at the Basilica of St Paul's outside the Walls, he stayed at the Venerable English College. I was a student there myself at the time. One evening he generously agreed to come upstairs to our common room to discuss any questions we students might want to raise with him. One of his remarks in particular has stuck in my memory. Asked what he regarded as the major obstacle to reunion, he answered that it was not in his view papal infallibility or the nature of authority in the Roman Church, but Mariology. And, if my memory is correct so many years later, the difficulty was not so much mariological doctrines, the immaculate conception and the assumption, as examples of the way ecclesiastical authority had been exercised, but rather the mariological issues in themselves.

By coincidence, one hundred years earlier – in January 1866, to be exact – Newman, recently restored to respect in the eyes of his fellow countrymen, both Anglican and Catholic, following his controversy with Charles Kingsley and the publication of his *Apologia pro Vita Sua*, had addressed a public *Letter* on this very subject to Edward Pusey, his lifelong friend since their days together in Oriel (see *Diff.* ii, pp. 1–170). I want to explore the more directly ecumenical implications of their correspondence later.[1]

---

1 See below, pp. 100–8.

Here it may be enough to observe that Newman had been prompted to write this *Letter* in response to a work by Pusey, his *Eirenicon*,[2] and, in doing so, as in his *Letter to the Duke of Norfolk* some years later with regard to papal infallibility, was taking the opportunity to offer a more moderate view of Mary as an alternative to the excesses common among some Catholics, like W. G. Ward and Frederick Faber. Their extremism created an obstacle for Anglicans. He wanted others to know, 'did they come to stand where I stand, what they would, and what they would not, be bound to hold concerning [the Blessed Virgin]!' (*Diff.* ii, p. 25). By helping others look towards Rome with more sympathy, he was addressing the very need to which Archbishop Ramsey was to draw attention in the English College a hundred years later.

(ii)

On 25 March 1832, the feast of the Annunciation, Newman preached a sermon called 'The Reverence due to the Blessed Virgin Mary' (see *P.S.* ii, pp. 127–38). He was thirty-one years old, he had yet to go on the Mediterranean holiday with the Froudes which was to have such an effect on him, and it was still more than a year before the Oxford Movement could be said to have begun. These were early days. Nevertheless, in this sermon he covered a remarkable range of teaching about Mary: for example, the annunciation made to her and her visit to her cousin, Elizabeth; then Mary as the second Eve; Mary as the mother of God's Son; Mary who as mother secures the true humanity of the child she bore; and when he referred also to her holiness and perfection, there were even those who accused him of holding the Roman Catholic doctrine of the immaculate conception. And there was more. All the same, in 1840, when struggling to preserve his place in the Church of England, following his crisis of the previous summer while reading about Monophysitism, he felt able

---

2 E. B. Pusey, *An Eirenicon in a Letter to the Author of 'The Christian Year'*, (Oxford, 1865).

to dismiss the notion that honour had been paid to Mary in the early Church. In an article which he was to call his 'last arrow' against Rome (*L.D.* vii, p. 418; see *Apo.* p. 134 [126]), he argued that there was no evidence of devotion to her among the apostles for there was no evidence of such devotion in the time immediately afterwards. It was incredible to suppose that the apostles would not have passed their devotion on (see *Ess.* ii, p. 15). Later, however, he changed his mind.

What made him change was his growing attention to early Church teaching. 'The Fathers made me a Catholic,' he told Pusey, 'and I am not going to kick down the ladder by which I ascended into the Church' (*Diff.* ii, p. 24). And in the early Church he discovered that Mary had often been called the second Eve. It seemed like the received teaching. He found it in the East in the writings of Justin Martyr, in the West in the writings of Tertullian, and he found it also in the writings of St Irenaeus, who spoke for both East and West since he came from Asia Minor and was a bishop in Gaul. He was the bishop of Lyons. In Newman's view, he also represented a tradition that went back through Polycarp to the Apostle, John. So when he reprinted his Anglican article as a Catholic, he noted his change of view: he observed that this teaching about Mary was so widespread in the period immediately after the apostles that it must have come from them (see *Ess.* ii, p. 15 n.). And he referred to his *Letter to Pusey* where he called this teaching 'rudimental', that is, 'the broad outline' from which a more perfect account would develop (*Diff.* ii, p. 31).

The basis of the teaching arises from seeing the scene of the human fall in the Garden of Eden as a drama involving three characters, the serpent, Adam, and Eve. And when the woman and the man were sentenced for their sin, God spoke to the serpent: 'I will put enmity between you and the woman, and between your offspring and hers; he will strike your head, and you will strike his heel' (Gen. 3:15). A future drama was being foretold. The scene would be re-enacted in which the serpent would meet a new Adam and a second Eve; and the new Adam would be the child, the offspring, of the new Eve.

The writings of Justin (*Dialogue with Trypho* 100), Tertullian (*L~Carne Christi* 17), and Irenaeus (*Adversus Haereses* 3:22, 34; 5:19), are full of the parallels and contrasts between Eve and Mary (see *Diff.* ii, pp. 33–5). Newman pointed them out and highlighted them: as Eve had co-operated in the fall of the human race, Mary co-operated in its salvation; as Eve had forfeited privileges by sin, Mary had earned privileges by grace; as Eve was disobedient and unbelieving, Mary was obedient and believing; as Eve was a cause of ruin to all, Mary was a cause of salvation to all; as Eve made room for Adam's fall, Mary made room for the redemption her Son won for us; and 'as Eve co-operated in effecting a great evil, Mary co-operated in effecting a much greater good' (see *Diff.* ii, p. 36). This way of arguing may be unfamiliar to us today, but it is difficult to resist the conclusion that these three authorities whom Newman used bore witness to a teaching more primitive than their own. As Newman remarked wryly, 'Only suppose there were so early and broad a testimony, to the effect that our Lord was a mere man, the son of Joseph; should we be able to insist upon the faith of the Holy Trinity as necessary to salvation?' (*Diff.* ii, p. 38). He then illustrated this teaching from seven more sources from the fourth and fifth centuries.[3]

This tradition, then, may be solid, but it may still seem odd to lay much stress on it today. Doesn't it look more like a relic of times past than a teaching which could be significant for the present? Writing to Pusey, however, Newman moved on from it boldly to concentrate 'upon two inferences, which it is obvious to draw from the rudimental teaching itself', Mary's sanctity and her dignity, or, in other words, her immaculate conception and her assumption into heaven (see *Diff.* ii, p. 44). As Eve was created in grace and her position as 'the Mother of all the living' indicated her dignity, how could Mary's state of grace and dignity be any less?

---

3 These were Cyril of Jerusalem, Ephrem, Epiphanius, Jerome, Augustine, Peter Chrysologus and Fulgentius (see *Diff.* ii. pp. 39–44).

Mary's sanctity

The doctrine of the immaculate conception was not new ground for Newman. In that early sermon in 1832 he had asked: 'What, think you, was the sanctity and grace of that human nature, of which God formed his sinless Son; knowing, as we do, "that what is born of the flesh, is flesh;" and that "none can bring a clean thing out of an unclean"?'[4] These were the words that had caused him to be 'accused of holding the doctrine of the Immaculate Conception'; for, as he explained in 1860 to Arthur Osborne Alleyne, a Catholic convert who had returned to Anglicanism, partly on account of his difficulty with this teaching, 'it was clear that I connected "grace" with the Blessed Virgin's humanity – as if grace and nature in her case never had been separated'. And he supported his view by referring to Justin, Tertullian and Irenaeus and the way they contrasted Mary and Eve as 'typical contrasts'(*L.D.* xix, pp. 346–7). Two weeks later he wrote Alleyne an extremely long letter which later he was to use when writing his *Letter to Pusey* (see *L.D.* xix, pp. 361–70). To Pusey he stated plainly that this teaching about the immaculate conception 'really does seem to me bound up in the doctrine of the Fathers, that Mary is the second Eve' (*Diff.* ii, p. 46).

It is not surprising then that when Newman wrote about the immaculate conception, he stressed the ease of accepting such a teaching, once due attention had been made to the condition of Eve. He pointed to a common view, Anglican as well as Catholic, that Eve's state was not of nature alone, but also of grace. And this grace was not something external, a favour or outward help, but an inward gift, given to Eve from the first moment of her personal

---

4 J. H. Newman, *Parochial Sermons* ii, 1st edition (London, 1835), p. 146. Later Anglican editions and the uniform edition were altered to read, 'What, think you, was the sanctified state of that human nature etc.?' See, for example, 4th edition, (London, 1843), p. 148, and *P.S.* ii, p. 132.

existence. And he asked, 'Is it possible to deny that Mary too had this gift from the very first moment of her personal existence?' That was what he understood the doctrine of the immaculate conception to imply, namely, Mary's possession of the inward gift of grace which gave her from the first that relationship with God which Eve had enjoyed at the first (see *Diff.* ii, pp. 45–6). He found it unavoidable that Mary must have been as fully endowed with grace as Eve. Had there been no fall, Newman observed, all Eve's children 'would have been conceived in grace, as in fact they were conceived in sin'. So Mary, he concluded, 'may be called, as it were, a daughter of Eve unfallen' (*Diff.* ii, p. 47).

One obvious difficulty with this approach concerns the legitimacy of contrasting the legendary Eve with the historical Mary. But even this problem may not be as intractable as it seems.

We need to remember that this contrast was never understood by Newman as something primarily historical. It was a contrast of type. Beyond a view of what might be thought actually to have happened, Eve was seen as a symbol of responsible co-operation in the fall of the human race and Mary symbolised responsible co-operation in its restoration. So it is not so much a question of accepting Eve as symbolic as coming to terms with the symbolic character of Mary's role. And in fact as scholars have come to realise how little they know about the historical Mary, so they have become more and more aware of her power as our pattern and example.

In his final University sermon, in which Newman sketched his theory of development in religious doctrine, inspired by the Lucan text which speaks of Mary pondering things in her heart (Luke 2:19), he stated that Mary 'symbolizes to us, not only the faith of the unlearned, but of the doctors of the Church also'. She stands as a model for all, the 'pattern of Faith, both in the reception and in the study of Divine Truth' (*U.S.* p. 313). She is seen as the one who has accomplished what each of us hopes to achieve. To say all this is obviously not to deny a historical basis for our understanding of Mary; what actually happened supplies the ground for the symbolism; to go no further, her title as the second Eve bears eloquent testimony to her reputation for holiness in the early Church. She was, to return to Newman's phrase, 'a daughter of Eve unfallen'.

That expression itself, however, may give rise to a further question. Did Newman mean that Mary was untouched by the fall, that she had no need of a saviour? The question turns on what is meant by original sin.

Radical Protestants have understood original sin as referring not merely to the human fall from grace and the dire consequences of that fall, but as an actual infection of human nature: original sin changed what it is to be human; thereafter we cannot avoid sinning. According to this interpretation, anyone who is unfallen, must, therefore, be a different kind of human being, essentially distinct from all those others who, left to themselves, can do nothing but sin. What need could such a person have of a saviour? Newman, however, held the Catholic view.

He explained that original sin does not permeate human nature, making all human acts sinful. It is instead something negative, depriving men and women of the grace which was originally given to Adam and Eve as a free gift. It enfeebles, but without contaminating. And so it is possible to be without sin in fact and therefore unfallen and, at the same time, to be a member of the fallen human race. That, according to Newman, was Mary's position.

He told Pusey:

> Protestants ... fancy that we ascribe a different nature from ours to the Blessed Virgin, different from that of her parents, and from that of fallen Adam. We hold nothing of the kind; we consider that in Adam she died, as others; that she was included with the whole human race in Adam's sentence; that she incurred his debt, as we do ... (*Diff.* ii, p. 48).

He was making the point that Mary's freedom from original sin did not set her apart in a different kind of human nature, because original sin has not become essential to being human. Moreover, her freedom from the debt of original sin she enjoyed because of her saviour, not in spite of him. Newman observed that, 'for the sake of Him who was to redeem her and us upon the Cross, to her the debt was remitted by anticipation, on her the sentence was not carried out, except indeed as regards her natural death, for she died when her time came, as others' (*Diff.* ii, p. 48). It was 'in order to fit her to become the Mother of her and our Redeemer, to fit her mentally, spiritually for it', that she received this 'special privilege' (*Diff.* ii, p. 49).

The very notion of privilege implies her share in our common, fallen nature. She *ought* to have been flawed as well. How else is her sinlessness privileged? On account of her role, Mary was preserved from original sin, while we are released from it. But the preserving and the releasing are no more than two expressions of the same redeeming work. She has had need of the Saviour as much as anyone.[5]

Mary's dignity

The arguments Newman used to explain Mary's assumption in his *Letter to Pusey* are much less likely to strike a chord today. He referred, for example, to the vision in the Apocalypse of the Woman and Child and asked whether the silence about Mary's dignity in the early Church was not evidence that it went unchallenged. He acknowledged that there were difficulties in the case he was making, but to us it may still seem too much like special pleading (see *Diff.* ii, pp. 50–61). All the same, he recognised that the image of the Woman pointed to the Church.

Then, three years later, as the First Vatican Council was beginning, the subject came up once more in a private letter to Magdalene Helbert who was attracted to Catholicism and corresponded with Newman, but she was received into the Catholic Church only shortly before she died. Newman told her that, were

5 Here too I readily acknowledge aspects of Newman's thought running through my account of the immaculate conception in *The Catholic Faith*, pp. 171–4.

the assumption to be defined at the Council, 'I should say that plainly it, as the Immaculate Conception, is contained in the dogma, "Mary the Second Eve – "', and he mentioned his *Letter to Pusey*. Then he went on: 'as to the Assumption, if Mary is like Eve but greater, then, as Eve would not have seen death or corruption, so, while Mary underwent death because she was a child of fallen Adam and sinned in Adam, she did not see corruption because she had more than the prerogatives of Eve' (*L.D.* xxiv, p. 330). Once again, the argument may not appeal to us, the explanation may seem too strained. Is there anything further to be added? I think there is.

In the long letter he wrote to Alleyne in 1860, which he used when preparing his *Letter to Pusey*, Newman early on made a remark which is germane here. He was referring to the immaculate conception, but the point touches the doctrine of the assumption as well. He was explaining the difference of view taken by Catholics and Protestants in these matters. He observed:

> Catholics do not view it [the immaculate conception] as a substantive and independent doctrine, so much as one of a family of doctrines which are intimately united together, whereas Protestants consider it as separate from every other, and as requiring a proof of its own as fully as if it were the only thing that we knew of the Blessed Virgin (*L.D.* xix, p. 362).

In other words, he was arguing that these doctrines are not to be assessed in isolation, but need rather to be seen in their relationship to others and to each other. Both the immaculate conception and the assumption are declarations of Mary's radical holiness in a very exact sense, a holiness, namely, which goes to the very roots of her existence.

They reveal, moreover, what our own redemption will be, when our sins have not only been forgiven, but destroyed. In the words of the English Dominican, Herbert McCabe, it shall be 'as though sin had never been. Redemption for us will involve a rebirth from an immaculate conception'. That radical holiness, which Mary's existence proclaims, is the destiny in which we hope to share: 'Her Assumption is the beginning of the resurrection of all who are taken up into Christ's resurrection.'[6] By drawing out inferences from her role as the second Eve, Newman himself becomes a witness to that belief in Mary's holiness which has been passed down, century after century. 'What height of glory may we not attribute to her?' he asked in his *Letter to Pusey*, just as, more than thirty years before, he had asked in that early sermon, 'Who can estimate the holiness and perfection of her, who was chosen to be the Mother of Christ?' (*Diff.* ii, p. 61; *P.S.* ii, p. 131).

(iv)

If anxiety about the doctrines of the immaculate conception and the assumption is one source of mariological controversy, another is the suspicion that praise offered to Mary distracts from the honour due to her Son. This problem surfaced in his *Letter to Pusey* when Newman examined her title as Mother of God, as Θεο–τοκος (*Theotokos, Deipara*).

When used in its approved sense, Newman explained, this word is neither rhetorical nor extravagant, but well-weighed, grave, and dogmatic: 'It intends to express that God is her Son, as truly as any one of us is the son of his own mother.' This title illustrates and brings together her holiness and her greatness: 'It is the issue of her sanctity; it is the origin of her greatness' (*Diff.* ii, p. 62). In fact a general review of Newman's thought about Mary would show that his understanding of her is founded firmly in his perception of her dignity as the Mother of her Son.[7]

None of this, of course, was disputed by Pusey. But this teaching about Mary as the Mother of God also inspired devotion to her. And that shift from teaching about her to devotion to her

---

6 Herbert McCabe, *God Matters*, (London, 1987), pp. 214, 213.

7 See Roderick Strange, 'The Development of Newman's Marian Thought and Devotion', *One in Christ* xvi (1980) 114–26.

was what made some people suspicious. As devotion grew, they became anxious. Pusey objected to Faber's words: 'Jesus is obscured, because Mary is kept in the background.'[8]

Newman, however, was not impressed by the objection. 'Now I say plainly,' he replied, 'I never will defend or screen any one from your just rebuke, who, through false devotion to Mary, forgets Jesus. But I should like the fact to be proved first; I cannot hastily admit it.' On the contrary, he argued, the evidence across Europe points in the other direction; 'just those nations and countries have lost their faith in the divinity of Christ, who have given up devotion to His Mother, and . . . those on the other hand, who have been foremost in her honour, have retained their orthodoxy' (*Diff.* ii, p. 92). Devotion to Mary safeguarded faith in the divinity of Christ.

I was reminded of this argument in 1977, when I found myself reading an article by Canon Donald Nicholson on 'Mary: a Living Tradition in Anglicanism'. He began:

> On 14 August 1927 I was present at an evening service in Wakefield Cathedral (Anglican). The preacher was the Chamberlain of York Minster and his theme was 'Mary', the next day being the 'illegal' feast of the Assumption. I remember his telling us that diminution in devotion to the Blessed Virgin was invariably followed by decline in belief in the divinity of Our Lord: unexpected and stirring words in those far-off days . . . .'[9]

And he drew to a close with words from a lecture by Bishop Eric Kemp of Chichester: 'The only reason for devotion to the Mother is that her Son is divine, and Marian devotion is a safeguard for the doctrine of the deity of Christ.' Canon Nicholson commented:

---

8 Pusey, *Eirenicon*, p. 118.
9 Donald Nicholson, 'Mary: a Living Tradition in Anglicanism', *The Clergy Review* lxii (1977) 318.

'What had been an *outré* remark on the lips of a minor canon fifty years ago becomes a considered judgment by a diocesan bishop of today.'[10] In the circumstances, it is difficult not to speculate on the spur for the Chamberlain's daring. Was he influenced by Newman's remark to Pusey? There may, of course, be no connection whatever, but the coincidence is at least noteworthy.

According to Newman, therefore, the doctrines of Mary's immaculate conception and her assumption bear witness to her radical holiness, while her title as Mother of God affirms her relationship with her Son and Saviour and proclaims her dignity. Moreover, as Newman declared to Pusey, once people 'recognize the sanctity and dignity of the Blessed Virgin', it is impossible for them not to perceive immediately that her role in heaven 'is one of perpetual intercession for the faithful' on earth (*Diff.* ii, p. 73). This well of holiness in her springs up on our behalf as intercession. Nevertheless, there can be misunderstandings. Intercession sounds so technical.

(v)

When we pray to Mary, people sometimes suppose that in this way too we are obscuring the honour due to her Son. Shouldn't we be praying to him, not to her? But there is a difference. Our prayer to God is invocation, we call on him; our prayer to Mary and the saints, and indeed to one another, is intercession, we are asking for help. The charming, rather earnest wife of an American evangelical pastor once challenged me on this very point: why did I pray to Mary, instead of praying to Jesus? I explained that Catholics do not really pray to her, but rather ask her to pray for them. The point was not immediately taken. So then I said, 'When you've a problem, don't you ask your husband to pray for you?' 'Of course, I do,' she replied at once. Then the penny dropped.

10 See Eric Kemp, *Mary and Right Belief in Christ*, (1975), quoted in Nicholson, 'Mary: a Living Tradition in Anglicanism', p. 322.

It is natural for Christians to pray for one another. We ask each other's help. And that is what intercession means. In particular we turn to those we admire, those who, we believe, lead good lives, people whom we judge to be holy. Holiness is the driving force of intercession (see *Diff.* ii, p. 71). That is why we ask for Mary's help. Her holiness commends her. She is not the source of mercy; we do not invoke her, as if she were divine; but she is our advocate (see *Diff.* ii, p. 101). We pray to her, ask for her help, trusting in her intercession. True devotion, properly understood, should cause no problems.

When it does, the cause is usually plain: devotion has become confused with doctrine. The vital distinction between them has been lost and, as a result, those with exaggerated views try to impose as essential doctrine their own favoured pious practices which at best are optional. Writing his *Letter to Pusey*, Newman also had his eye on these Catholics. The antidote was to maintain firmly the distinction between doctrine and devotion. Newman emphasised its importance (see *Diff.* ii, p. 97; *L.D.* xxii, p. 90). When that was secure, it would restrain this devotional dogmatism and release that authentic devotion which is the natural consequence of deep faith.

At the same time, he was also aware of something even worse, the excesses which had appalled Pusey and which he too regarded as scandalous. He attacked them without mercy. He summarised a whole range of them, for example, 'that the Blessed Virgin is superior to God', 'that Christ fulfilled the office of Saviour by imitating her virtues', and 'that His Body and Blood in the Eucharist are truly hers and appertain to her'. Those views, he stated,

> seem to me like a bad dream ... They do but scare and confuse me. I should not be holier, more spiritual, more sure of perseverance, if I twisted my moral being into the reception of them; ... I will have nothing to do with statements [about Mary], which can only be explained, by being explained away.

And he dismissed these excesses as 'calculated to prejudice inquirers, to frighten the unlearned, to unsettle consciences, to provoke blasphemy, and to work the loss of souls' (*Diff.* ii, pp. 113–15).

(vi)

If deep faith in Mary, as Newman observed, soon inspired true devotion, it seems natural to ask about his own devotion to her. He explained his position in a private letter to Pusey in 1865.

There he confirmed his conviction that anyone entering a Church like himself should take up its practical system, 'its popular catechisms and books of devotion'. All the same, he insisted upon a distinction between this system and 'the additions or colour which it receives in this country or that, in this class, in this school, or that' (*L.D.* xxii, p. 100). These remarks merely echoed the position he ascribed to himself in his *Apologia*. Certain extravagant continental devotions in Mary's honour had been, he confessed, his 'great *crux* as regards Catholicism'. He went on: 'I say frankly, I do not fully enter into them now; I trust I do not love her the less, because I cannot enter into them. They may be fully explained and defended; but sentiment and taste do not run with logic: they are suitable for Italy, but they are not suitable for England' (*Apo.* p. 195 [176–7]). His own spiritual temperament, he added, shaped his disposition, that intense awareness of the divine presence – of himself and his Creator as the two absolute and luminously self-evident beings – made any extravagance unthinkable (see *Apo.* pp. 195, 4 [177, 18].

He made his position plain in the *Letter* he published: 'May God's mercy keep me from the shadow of a thought, dimming the purity or blunting the keenness of that love of Him, which is our sole happiness and our sole salvation!' What then of Mary? She is 'only our Mother by divine appointment, given us from the Cross; her presence is above, not on earth; her office is external, not within us ... her power is indirect. It is her prayers that avail, and her prayers are effectual by the *fiat* of Him who is our all in all'

(*Diff.* ii, pp. 83–4). If those words seem restrained, they should not be mistaken for a lack of true devotion.[11] True devotion is warm, generous, and free; it defies criticism (see *Diff.* ii, p. 80). However, it must never become the slave of extravagance. For Newman it never did.

It seems to me that Newman's appeal to the Fathers, his awareness of the distinction between doctrine and devotion, while recognising their relationship, his attention to Mary's holiness and dignity, and his hostility to excess are all points of ecumenical significance. Let me return to Archbishop Ramsey.

(vii)

A week after his meeting with Pope Paul VI in 1966, Dr Ramsey visited Newman's Oxford College, Oriel, to open a Symposium in Newman's honour. He suggested that renewal for both Anglicans and Catholics would come from recapturing something of Newman's spirit, which he characterised as the spirit of scriptural holiness. That holiness is the basis of Christian unity.[12] Moreover, its outstanding model, we may add, is the mother of Jesus.

In an early Catholic letter, Newman acknowledged his debt to Mary: 'I have ever been under her shadow, if I may say it. My College was St Mary's, and my Church; and when I went to Littlemore, there, by my previous disposition, our Blessed Lady was waiting for me' (*L.D.* xii, pp. 153–4). And so it was. Oriel is formally St Mary's College; the University Church where Newman was vicar is the church of St Mary the Virgin; and his church at Littlemore is dedicated to St Mary the Virgin and St Nicholas. Shortly after writing this letter, he named his Oratory Church in Birmingham after her immaculate conception. He remained under her shadow to the end.

---

11 See also Bishop William Ullathorne's letter to the editor of *The Tablet* in *L.D.* xxii, pp. 341–4, on Newman's devotion to the Blessed Virgin.

12 See A. M. Ramsey, 'The Significance of Newman Today', in John Coulson and A. M. Allchin (eds.) *The Rediscovery of Newman*, (London, 1967), p. 8.

6

Serving the Laity

(i)

When the Second Vatican Council began on 11 October 1962, there were those who did not expect it to last very long, perhaps no more than a single session. They realised that the documents that had been prepared for the assembled bishops would no doubt be amended, but they were quite confident that they would also be approved. The Council would be over very soon. That expectation, however, was not fulfilled. Many bishops were critical of the documents, their content and their character. And beyond that there was something else. It took almost the full eight weeks of that first session to articulate it: what had been prepared was too diffuse; it needed focus. On 2 December 1962, the Archbishop of Milan, Cardinal Giovanni Battista Montini, who barely six months later would become Pope Paul VI, wrote to his diocesan newspaper, *L'Italia*. He described this session as a running-in period. Nevertheless, it had served its purpose. These weeks, he concluded, had helped the Council identify its central theme: 'the Church'.[1] Three days later he made the same point in the Council chamber.

As the Council Fathers explored that theme more closely, they came to concentrate less on an approach which understood the Church principally in terms of what distinguished its members from each other, in other words, its hierarchical structure, and gave priority instead to what united them, their common baptism. This was the source from which the revival of the understanding

---

1 See Peter Hebblethwaite, *John XXIII, Pope of the Council*, (London, 1984), p. 461.

of the Church as κοινωνία (*koinōnia* or communion) sprang.
Emphasis was placed on the unity of all the faithful and it meant,
therefore, that the lay faithful came into their own. There is a
rather clumsy sentence in the eventual Decree on the Lay Apostolate: 'Within christian communities [the laity's] activity is so
necessary that without it the pastors' apostolate cannot generally
(*plerumque*) attain its full effect' (*Apostolicam Actuositatem*, no. 10). It
may be read in a highly clerical way, as though the poor laity are
simply topping up what the clergy have not managed to achieve
on their own; in fact, however, it is pointing to the essential need
for activity in the Church to be properly integrated.

As this awareness of the lay apostolate emerged, there were
those who saw Newman as one of its pioneers. They pointed in
particular to the article he had written for *The Rambler* in 1859,
'On Consulting the Faithful in Matters of Doctrine'. It had caused
him trouble then; now it was being recognised as prophetic.[2] We
must consider it. But it would be a mistake to see that one article as
somehow an isolated instance in Newman's life and work. His
commitment to the laity and the service he gave them was profound and lifelong.

(ii)

Newman's Oxford, of course, was predominantly clerical. The
university he knew both as an undergraduate and as a don was
largely in the charge of unmarried clergymen. Only the heads of
the colleges could be married. When a young don, who would
usually have been ordained, decided to marry, he had to resign his
fellowship and seek a parish living. There were many in the gift of
the colleges.

As we have noticed already, however, even at an early age
Newman's pastoral instinct made him sensitive to the influence of

---

2 See the edition produced by John Coulson in 1961; it was reprinted in
   1986; John Coulson (ed.), *John Henry Newman: On Consulting the Faithful in
   Matters of Doctrine*, (London, 1961, 1986).

those among whom he found himself. [3] He went to his first curacy at St Clement's as an earnest evangelical Anglican, but his stern viewpoint was softened by the sheer goodness of the people he met there. It was not possible for him to believe that most of them would be damned. He was attentive to his parishioners as they really were. Then, as a tutor at Oriel, he saw his duty as extending beyond intellectual instruction; there was a moral dimension as well. Those who were hostile viewed this approach as theological indoctrination, but others compared it to the attention only given to pupils by the very best private tutors. [4] Afterwards, when the Oxford Movement was at its height while he was Vicar of St Mary the Virgin, the University Church, he delivered his *Lectures on the Prophetical Office* and afterwards his *Lectures on Justification*. These were not formal university lectures, but were given in the Adam de Brome chapel in St Mary's to deepen the understanding of those who attended them. And then again the scope and style of his *Parochial Sermons* should not be forgotten. Moreover, while Vicar of St Mary's, he had the parish church built at Littlemore, the place which was to become so important to him, as he struggled to determine his future between Canterbury and Rome and where he wrote his *Essay on Development*. On my first visit there in 1966, I was shown around by a woman whose grandfather as a young boy had heard Newman preach his last Anglican sermon there in 1843. He had moved those who heard him by speaking about 'The Parting of Friends' (see *S.D.* pp. 395–409). All these activities, integral to his Anglican life, point to his commitment to serving lay people. They also bear witness to his later assertion – one of those recurring themes or preoccupations, which shaped his life – that education had always been his line (see *A.W.* p. 259).

Then, besides these features of his Anglican life, the vocation he chose as a Catholic priest also has a bearing on his approach to the laity. When he was sent to Rome to prepare for ordination, he was

---

3 See above, pp. 6–7.
4 See A. J. Engel, *From Clergyman to Don: the Rise of the Academic Profession in Nineteenth-Century Oxford*, (Oxford, 1983), p. 25.

unsure what kind of priest he ought to be. He wondered about becoming a Jesuit or a Dominican, a Vincentian or Redemptorist; but he found himself drawn in fact by the person of St Philip Neri.

Philip had been born in Florence in 1515, but he came to Rome as a young man. He lived simply and helped people generously. They were attracted by the warmth and gentleness of his personality. His ministry became so effective that he was recognised as the apostle of Rome for his own time. Some of those who were influenced by him gathered to join him in prayer in the small oratory in the Church of San Girolamo della Carità. These, of course, were largely lay people. When these meetings began, Philip was still a layman himself. When he was ordained eventually in 1551, he and those who had gathered with him who were also priests became known as Oratorians. Although they lived in community, they were secular priests. They took no vows and were able to keep their own possessions. Philip was not interested in eye-catching display. His ideal was 'to love to be unknown' (see *O.S.* p. 241). This was the model of priestly life and ministry that caught Newman's heart and imagination. In many ways it reflected and recreated for him as a Catholic priest the life in community with unmarried clergymen which he had cherished as a fellow of Oriel. And their Birmingham parish also meant that he continued the ministry he had exercised in Oxford and at Littlemore.

The bond that bound Oratorians together was one of love and a sense of family, rather than the rule of authority and obedience. That aspect also was in tune with Newman's capacity for friendship.

There is a kind of paradox here. He was sometimes described as a man who was never less alone than when alone; there was something reserved and solitary about him. All the same, he had an extraordinary gift for friendship. His many letters bear witness to that and those, for example, to the women who were his friends, illustrate the fact beyond dispute.[5] Then in his poem, 'A

5 See Joyce Sugg, *Ever Yours Affly: John Henry Newman and his Female Circle*, (Leominster, 1996).

Thanksgiving', written in October 1829, he spoke of 'Blessings of friends, which to my door/ Unask'd, unhoped, have come' (*V.V.* p. 46). Newman saw in friendship love made real. He was not persuaded that it is better to love everyone in general. When he preached about the beloved disciple two years later, he saw in the friendship between Jesus and John an example to follow. He stated his conviction that 'the best preparation for loving the world at large, and loving it duly and wisely, is to cultivate an intimate friendship and affection towards those who are immediately about us' (*P.S.* ii, pp. 52–3).

Here too I gladly and gratefully acknowledge Newman's influence on me. These words struck a chord when I first read them many years ago. And now, looking back, I wonder how I could have survived my long years of celibate priesthood without my friends. There are, of course, those nowadays who can make no sense of such relationships, uncluttered by physical sexual activity. They doubt whether they actually exist. But they do. Just as the best marriages are often built as much on friendship as on passion, so many of us who are single, whether by choice or chance or commitment to celibacy, know what it means to delight in our friends. I have paid tribute to mine elsewhere and am happy to do so again. They offer me 'a promise of merriment, good talk, wise advice, and generous hospitality ... I hold them in love and believe I am loved by them. They do not diminish the ministry I offer. They are pure gift for which I give constant thanks.'[6] As well as my own experience, Newman's conviction also underlies these words. We cannot love in general unless we love in particular.

And, while he loved his friends, he valued marriage too. On 12 January 1854, preaching at the religious profession as a Visitation nun of Mary Anne Bowden, the daughter of John Bowden who had died in 1844, but who had been his friend since they were undergraduates together at Trinity College, Oxford, he spoke powerfully of her religious calling, but not before he had spoken also of marriage as the 'one central and supreme attachment to

6 Roderick Strange, *The Risk of Discipleship*, (London, 2004), p. 161.

which none other can be compared'. These words are full of power. Children leave parents, he went on, as Jesus left Mary, but marriage is indestructible and recalls 'the everlasting ineffable love with which the Father loves the Son who is in His bosom and the Son the Father who has from all eternity begotten Him'.[7] If these words seem fanciful and unrealistic in a society scarred by marital breakdown, we ought still to be able to recognise the ideal.

His pastoral ministry as an Anglican, his Oratorian vocation, and his valuing of friendship and marriage as paths to fulfilling the great commandment of love, all point to the context within which his service of lay people was realised. That service was plain in his Catholic years, in particular during his time as Rector of the University he established in Dublin and then afterwards during the brief, but turbulent, period when he was editor of *The Rambler*. In themselves these two episodes are distinct, but they can also be connected.

(iii)

On 21 January 1863 there is an entry in Newman's Journal which still makes sombre reading. He was chronicling his life since he had become a Catholic in 1845 and he was perhaps at his lowest point. The mood is dark, even depressive. He acknowledged how little he personally seemed to have done as a Catholic. It was said, for example, that Manning and Faber made converts, but he did not. However, he was reluctant, as he put it, 'to make hasty converts of educated men, lest they should not have counted the cost, and should have difficulties after they have entered the Church' (see *A.W.* pp. 257–8). And he went on to lament the condition of Catholics in England, who 'from their very blindness, cannot see that they are blind'. Newman's wish was to help them assess the arguments they took for granted and examine their position with regard to the culture of the day; then, as their views developed, they would intellectually become more mature. In other words, he

---

7 Murray (ed.), *Newman the Oratorian*, p. 275.

wanted to educate them. This was the particular place where he declared that education, that fourth major preoccupation or theme, was his 'line': 'Now from first to last, education, in this large sense of the word, has been my line' (*A.W.* p. 259).

This concern for education was evident most dramatically in his work to found the Catholic University in Dublin. He had been invited to go there in 1851. Earlier that very year, quite independently, he had articulated his ideal: 'I want a laity, not arrogant, not rash in speech, not disputatious, but men who know their religion, who enter into it, who know just where they stand, who know what they hold, and what they do not, who know their creed so well, that they can give an account of it, who know so much of history that they can defend it.' These words resonate deeply with me. The text of my book, *The Catholic Faith*, which was published in 1986 while I was a chaplain at Oxford, I forced myself to write by preparing the chapters first as lectures. The lecture series was called 'An Account of Catholicism'. And I spoke and wrote for the same purpose as Newman. I can make his words my own: 'I want an intelligent, well-instructed laity' (*Prepos.* p. 390). I was aware of questions raised by students, whether Catholic or not, by an older generation, curious about or bewildered by the Second Vatican Council, and a still older generation who had never been prepared for change at all. Each in their different ways had urgent needs. It was Newman's preoccupation, but in my own setting.

The invitation to go to Dublin had come to Newman from Archbishop Paul Cullen of Armagh who soon afterwards was transferred to Dublin and later made a Cardinal. Newman gave himself to the project with great generosity for seven years.

The plan itself had been proposed by the Irish bishops as an alternative to the Queen's Colleges which Robert Peel had established in Ireland. These colleges were unacceptable to the bishops because they excluded all religious teaching and they were open to the members of any Church and to non-believers alike. Oxford and Cambridge, on the other hand, still imposed religious tests at that time which made them at least in principle unavailable

to Catholics. Here then was an opportunity to create a Catholic
university for Catholics from the entire English-speaking world.
Newman had hopes of students coming from America as well as
England. He had in mind a kind of Oxford ideal transposed to the
banks of the Liffey. 'Curious it will be', as he observed to his
friend, Catherine Froude, 'if Oxford is imported into Ireland'
(*L.D.* xiv, p. 389). He was also keen to have lay professors and in
the event twenty-seven of the thirty-two he appointed were
laymen.

However, it proved to be a heartbreaking exercise. The Irish
bishops had something much less ambitious in view, more a
Catholic training college than a university. And they disagreed
among themselves. At the same time, Newman found Cullen
more and more difficult to work with. As demands were also
increasing in Birmingham, he resigned finally in 1858 and
returned to his Oratory.

A considerable literature has grown up around this initiative. At
the heart of it is what many people have regarded as a masterpiece,
Newman's discourses on university education, which he published
as *The Idea of a University*. His biographies examine it, there have
been specialist studies, discussions, and controversies about it, and
in 1976 Ian Ker produced his masterly critical edition. It is not
necessary or practicable to examine those matters again here. But
there are some points worth considering which have a more
immediate bearing on Newman's service of the laity.

It is natural to ask, for example, whether his *Idea of a University*
still has something to offer us today. It was the question examined
by John Roberts in 1990, the centenary of Newman's death. He
revisited Newman's discourses and was ideally equipped to do so.[8]
A leading British historian, Roberts, who died in 2003, had also
been Vice-Chancellor of Southampton University and then, from

---

8 See J. M. Roberts, '*The Idea of a University* Revisited', in Ker and Hill (eds.),
   Newman after a Hundred Years, pp. 193–222. For a related, but more positive
   view, see Nicholas Lash, '"A Seat of Wisdom, a Light of the World":
   Considering the University', *Louvain Studies* xv (1990) 188–202.

1984 to 1994, he was Warden of Merton College, Oxford. He had been in the thick of the educational debate in recent times.

So does Newman's *Idea* still have something to offer us? Roberts was not easily persuaded. While he acknowledged the subtlety of Newman's style, his carefully qualified arguments which are often more nuanced than they may seem at first, he felt that our circumstances today are too different, 'utterly remote from the academic world taken for granted by Newman' (p. 198). Who could disagree? We may, for instance, still like to see knowledge as an end in itself, but much that goes on in universities now 'is consciously a means to useful ends', training for a career (p. 201). Newman was far removed from that attitude and from 'the realities of modern universities urged by society to give greater attention to the social utility of their "outputs"' (pp. 202–3). Then again, Newman held that universities should in principle teach all branches of knowledge (see *Idea*, p. [440]), yet what he was wanting, Roberts observed, is in practice 'impossible' (pp. 204–5). And in any case our fragmented, post-modern society is very different from the integrated vision of society with its unchanging values in which Newman believed. And there is more. We don't need to review it all here. In brief, Roberts was saying, universities nowadays have developed in ways very different from the one Newman envisaged.

So has he, therefore, nothing to offer us? But that would not be true either. There is something. Roberts described it as 'a vision with which those of us who are concerned with education should from time to time try to refresh ourselves'. He noted that, while we should not strive to force Newman's *Idea* to fit our needs, we can still be inspired and stimulated by it. His vision can encourage us 'to defend values now under threat'. And Roberts went on: 'It is helpful to recall that an educated man is not a man who knows certain things, but a man whose mind has been formed in a certain way and who can take up a certain stance when confronted with a new experience' (pp. 221–2). Newman and his contemporaries were often formidably learned; they knew a very great deal; in today's terms, they were strong on content; but beyond content they excelled at competence.

So, if Newman's vision is to be respected, it is also important to recognise it for what it is, to be aware of its limitations, as he was. Liberal education produces the gentleman. In the *Idea*, Newman offered a description of such a person which has become well-known. There is much to be admired: 'a cultivated intellect, a delicate taste, a candid, equitable, dispassionate mind, a noble and courteous bearing in the conduct of life'. Those qualities are the fruit of the liberal education Newman was championing. All the same, he declared, 'they are no guarantee for sanctity or even for conscientiousness' (*Idea*, pp. 120–121 [110]). That was his concern. Greater knowledge, deeper learning, admirable in themselves, cannot ensure moral improvement. And he reinforced his point with unforgettable images: 'Quarry the granite rock with razors, or moor the vessel with a thread of silk; then may you hope with such keen and delicate instruments as human knowledge and human reason to contend against those giants, the passion and the pride of man' (*Idea*, p. 121 [111]). Newman needed something more for his Catholic University.

What he wanted, in his desire for an education that would be at the service of the laity, was a relationship between intellectual excellence and religious commitment in which they were both truly at one, united, while they maintained their distinct integrity. He set out this viewpoint in the first of a series of sermons he preached in Dublin in 1856 and 1857.

He dismissed out of hand the charge that by advocating this union between intellect and religion he was countenancing censorship, 'ecclesiastical supervision' of intellectual matters. Nor was he interested in compromise, as though each partner had to yield something. 'I wish the intellect to range with the utmost freedom, and religion to enjoy an equal freedom', he declared. His driving concern was personal. He wanted what was intellectual and what was religious to be properly integrated within the same individual. 'It will not satisfy me, what satisfies so many,' he explained, 'to have two independent systems, intellectual and religious, going at once side by side, by a sort of division of labour, and only accidentally brought together.' He was utterly opposed to any such division. And he summed up his ideal: 'I want the intellectual layman to be religious, and the devout ecclesiastic to be intellectual' (see *O.S.* p. 13).

In a later sermon in the same series, Newman took up this theme again. He did so by dividing saints into two categories. There are those, he said, who are 'so absorbed in the divine life', that they seem altogether disconnected from human life and its affairs, and then there are others 'in whom the supernatural combines with nature, instead of superseding it'. In them, grace invigorates, elevates, and ennobles nature. They are 'not the less men, because they are saints'. And he continued: 'The world is to them a book, to which they are drawn for its own sake, which they read fluently, which interests them naturally, - though, by the reason of the grace which dwells within them, they study it and hold converse with it for the glory of God and the salvation of souls' (*O.S.* pp. 91–3). Newman certainly admired the first group, but he was inspired by the second.

This is the vision that also has inspired me. It looks to Jesus of Nazareth as the one who was as truly divine as he was truly human, as truly human as he was truly divine. And so, as a university chaplain, I would urge members of the university that our share in Christ's life must not be at the expense of our humanity. 'Our spirituality and our living witness must engage with our world, our surroundings, our conditions. In that sense, it is not enough to be in the world, but not of it; we have to be both in the world *and of the world*. As aliens, we can never reclaim it. We have to be at home here if we are to bear witness effectively.'[9] And as a seminary rector I have insisted that we need to discover the identity of those who are ordained through recognising their place within the community, not by simply setting them apart.[10] I acknowledge Newman's influence.

In Dublin, therefore, although he spoke of 'the idea' of a university, Newman was not simply laying out a master plan, a

9 Strange, *Living Catholicism*, pp. 125–6.
10 See Strange, *The Risk of Discipleship*, pp. 50–3.

Platonic ideal of university education at large, but more particularly he was responding to the demands of his own circumstances
there, and encouraging a vision in which intellectual training,
moral discipline, and religious commitment are combined. It was
not a vision which he found easy to make real. He was constantly
frustrated and eventually he resigned as Rector on 12 November
1858.

(iv)

Once he was settled back in Birmingham, however, he was soon
disturbed again. He was drawn into the crisis surrounding *The
Rambler* which many people regarded as the finest Catholic periodical of its kind in the English-speaking world. But the bishops
were becoming increasingly impatient with its more liberal tone.
They were irritated especially by its editor, Richard Simpson, who
was a good man and a devoted Catholic, but someone who was
also unafraid of criticising them. They were not amused. Some of
them wanted to censure the paper in their pastoral letters. To
avoid that and the scandal it might cause, Newman's bishop,
Ullathorne, asked Newman, first of all, to persuade Simpson to
resign. And Newman, who was friendly with Simpson, was able
to do so. But then the question arose about a successor. Who
was to be editor in Simpson's place? It had to be someone
acceptable both to *The Rambler's* proprietors and to the bishops. It
quickly became clear that Newman himself was the obvious
choice. And his very commitment to serving the laity, to their
education in the broad and deep sense which had also guided his
work in Dublin, led him to accept.

Newman too, like Ullathorne, had been critical at times of
Simpson's tone. Nevertheless, he liked him and shared his principles. In the first issue for which he was responsible, therefore, in
May 1859, he wrote positively about the importance of consulting
the laity in something which concerned them closely. The issue
was the controversy at that time about the lack of Catholic
representation on the Royal Commission on elementary

education. The Catholic Poor Schools Committee had probably been at fault, but Simpson had seemed critical of the way the bishops had handled the matter. That was a significant feature of the crisis which had prompted his removal. Newman in his first issue dealt with the bishops generously; he made it plain that no disrespect towards them had been intended. But he was not prepared to let the matter pass without comment. He also observed: 'If even in the preparation of a dogmatic definition the faithful are consulted, as lately in the instance of the Immaculate Conception [in 1854], it is at least as natural to anticipate such an act of kind feeling and sympathy in great practical questions', such as education (see *L.D.* xix, p. 129, n.3). He apologised if the words used before or their tone seemed disrespectful, but went on to argue that there was no disrespect in assuming that the bishops would want to know the views of the laity on so great a question.

He was wrong. And his carefully chosen words provoked Dr John Gillow, a priest on the staff of the seminary at Ushaw College, near Durham, to protest. Gillow regarded the notion that the laity might be consulted in matters of doctrine as virtually heresy. He and Newman exchanged courteous letters and the point at issue between them was settled, although it flared again later. But opposition to *The Rambler* in certain quarters was relentless.

Ullathorne himself had become uncomfortable with the direction affairs were taking and called on Newman at the Oratory to discuss the situation on 22 May. This was the well-known occasion when, according to Newman's memorandum of their meeting, Ullathorne at one point asked him, 'Who are the laity?' And Newman answered 'that the Church would look foolish without them – *not* those words' (*L.D.* xix, p. 141). During the conversation he also remarked to Ullathorne that it would in fact be a relief to give up *The Rambler* and to his surprise Ullathorne encouraged him to do so. It was not a command, more a suggestion, but one which Ullathorne made eagerly. And so Newman decided that he would resign. He could not do so immediately, of course. He had to take responsibility for one more issue, due for July, and he decided to use the opportunity to explore further the issue which Gillow had challenged. That was his reason for writing his article, *On Consulting the Faithful in Matters of Doctrine*. It is packed with examples about the bishops in the fourth century who had largely caved in to the heresy known as Arianism, while the lay faithful resisted it. In this outstanding instance, their fidelity had safeguarded the faith of the Church.

The immediate consequences for Newman personally were painful. Those who opposed him complained to Rome. He was accused of undermining the teaching authority of the bishops. Rome asked for an explanation and he was ready to offer one, but Rome's specific questions were not passed on to him. Silence, therefore, ensued. While he thought all was well, Rome thought he had refused its request. Little by little, Newman became aware that something was amiss. In the midst of the gloom, during that dark period in his life, he composed a memorandum about *The Rambler* affair on 28 November 1862. One sentence reads: 'All would have been well, but for the unlucky paragraph in my July Number on the Arianizing Hierarchy' (*L.D.* xix, p. 151). The matter was not resolved until 1867, when his friend and fellow-Oratorian, Ambrose St John, visited Rome. The incident is typical of Newman's fortunes at that time. We do not need to discuss it further. It has been examined thoroughly elsewhere.[11] All the same, we should notice the core of Newman's position, what he understood consulting the laity to mean. It may guide us still. He identified five points in particular.[12]

What had roused Gillow was Newman's specific reference to consulting the laity in preparing a dogmatic definition. In the panegyric at his funeral, Gillow's lectures and replies to questions were described as having 'all the precision and cogency of a mathematical problem'.[13] To someone with such a way of thinking, Newman's words, as he told him in the letter he wrote

---

11 See in particular, John Coulson, *Newman and the Common Tradition*, (Oxford, 1970), pp. 113–31.

12 See Coulson (ed.), *On Consulting*, pp. 73–5.

13 Quoted in the note on John Gillow in *L.D.* xix, p. 586.

on 15 May, implied that 'the infallible portion [of the Church] would consult the fallible with a view to guiding itself to an infallible decision' (see *L.D.* xix, p. 134, n.3). But Newman in his answer insisted that that view misread his meaning. He was speaking of consulting as it is used in English every day, not principally as asking an opinion, but rather to discover a fact. That was the first point he identified. He offered the example of 'consulting a barometer about the weather. The barometer does not give us its opinion, but ascertains for us a fact'. And he held his ground, refusing to concede to Gillow that infallibility lies exclusively in the teaching Church. He drew on the authority of the Jesuit theologian, Giovanni Perrone, whom he had known in Rome in 1847, to argue that infallibility resides in both those who teach and those who are taught; they are as one, 'as a figure is contained both on the seal and on the wax' (*L.D.* xix, pp. 135–6). And the laity are consulted as witnesses so that their mind may be known. He made the same point again years later during the First Vatican Council (see *L.D.* xxv, p. 172).

The second point Newman identified was what he called 'a sort of instinct, or φρονημα, deep in the bosom of the mystical body of Christ'. This instinct may be hard to define, but is not so difficult to recognise. It corresponds to what he would call the illative sense in his *Grammar of Assent*.[14] Years earlier, in one of his university sermons, he had referred to it implicitly when he noted how in practical matters, 'when their minds are really roused, men commonly are not bad reasoners' (*U.S.* p. 211). We have an instinct for the right way to proceed. Whether we are 'gifted or not', we have an inward faculty. It inspired another of his unforgettable images. He likened this inward faculty to skilful mountaineering, making progress like 'a clamberer on a steep cliff, who, by quick eye, prompt hand, and firm foot, ascends how he knows not himself, by personal endowments and by practice, rather than by rule, leaving no track behind him, and unable to teach another' (*U.S.* p. 257). Newman had confidence in human reason.

14 See above, pp. 29–30.

All the same, there is an obvious question. Such an instinct may be identified in individuals, but can it be found in communities? Many would be sceptical, but I am not. Think of the communities you know, the groups to which you belong. For years, while living in Oxford, I would see visitors on guided tours being shown around the University. They would be taken into many colleges and admire them. But by the evening I suspect it had all become a bit of a blur. They could not remember how to distinguish between Exeter, Lincoln and Jesus, or Trinity and St John's, or Corpus and Oriel. They all seemed the same. But to the members of those colleges their distinctiveness was evident. Each community has its own character, its own identity, and its own self-understanding. And so the Church. The larger the community, the more complex the exercise, investigating and exploring, but the reality is the same. There is a mind that can be determined.

And the witness of the laity which consultation determines and the instinctive, inward faculty which articulates it, emerges, Newman explained, in part under the direction of the Holy Spirit and partly as an answer to prayer. These are the third and fourth points he identified. The authentic life of the community derives from the Spirit dwelling within believers, who are sensitive to and respond to what they have received. This is not cheap grace, but the fruit of costly commitment. Then what they perceive becomes known in their prayer, not as the canonising of casual whims, but the result of painstaking discernment.

Such authentic life in the community displays one further characteristic, the fifth point in the process which Newman was explaining. He called it 'jealousy of error'. Put simply, we may say that, where life is authentic, it realises very soon when something has gone wrong. We see it sometimes physically in surgery, to use an example which could never have occurred to Newman: when an organ has been transplanted, heart or kidney, there is the danger of rejection. And in general, when opinions or decisions are proposed to it as its own, a community will recognise almost at once when they are not. The discord will be evident.

That in brief was what Newman meant by consulting the laity.

It was a process designed to determine what the community believed in fact, based on the confidence that it knew its own mind. That confidence was all the more secure because the lay faithful lived a life rooted in the Spirit to whom they were responsive in prayer. And such a spiritual life was impatient of error, it would recognise very soon what did not ring true.

Newman then went on to illustrate the part played by lay witness in the history of the Church and at the end of his article he concluded that 'each constituent portion of the Church has its proper functions, and no portion can be safely neglected ... there is something in the "pastorum et fidelium *conspiratio*," which is not in the pastors alone'. He was emphasising the value of what was done in common and he argued that the clergy should seek to encourage the lay faithful, otherwise, he observed, if they cut them off from the study of doctrine and from contemplation, and required from them only 'a *fides implicita*', then that unthinking acceptance, 'in the educated classes will terminate in indifference, and in the poorer in superstition'.[15] People need to be involved, to contribute, to recognise the part they have to play.

It was the natural conclusion from what he had just illustrated, but it was a startling conclusion for those days, when the laity were regarded as 'boys eternal',[16] and the accepted atmosphere breathed clericalism and condescension. We, however, can see in it a modest anticipation of that emphasis on the unity of all the baptized which was to gain such recognition at Vatican II.

(v)

Newman's entire life, both Anglican and Catholic, was devoted to the service of the lay faithful. And during his Catholic life he tried to serve the laity in many ways besides his work in Dublin and his editing of *The Rambler*. He founded, for example, the Oratory School which was a great labour and also caused him much

15 Coulson (ed.), *On Consulting*, pp. 103–4, 106.
16 See Coulson, *Newman and the Common Tradition*, p. 96.

heartache at times; and his attempt also to establish an Oratory in Oxford was driven by the same concern, to be of service to Catholics there. However, I have concentrated here on these two episodes in particular, his work for the University in Dublin where he tried to establish a way of offering the lay faithful a deeper, fuller education, and his experience as editor of *The Rambler* where he championed and tried to defend their role. Both episodes caused him great sorrow. Neither can be regarded as a clear success at the time. But let me leave the final word to John Coulson:

> Newman's abiding vision was that, in the dark days that were approaching and have now inevitably come upon us, the fullness of the Catholic idea demanded that the intellectual layman become religious and the devout ecclesiastic intellectual. He had hoped that it was his vocation to bring about the means by which this might be achieved – by his University, his school, his house at Oxford, and his support for the work of *The Rambler*. But it was not to be so. His was that greater vocation still: to witness, by the way in which he met and mastered the indifference, hostility, persecution and tardy recognition of his Catholic life to the very embodiment of that ideal he had devoted his life to foster: the practice of the saintly intellect.[17]

17 Coulson (ed.), introduction to *On Consulting*, pp. 47–8.

7

Seeking Church Unity

(i)

In the library of the Venerable English College, Rome, there is a scrapbook, filled with articles cut out of newspapers which feature former members of the College. Many had become bishops or held other responsible positions in the Church. As a student there in the 1960s, I used to enjoy browsing through it. The earlier pieces, going back decades, frequently told stories of clashes between these former students and their Anglican or Free Church counterparts. The tone was combative, often abrasive. But then there was a change. Soon after the election of Pope John XXIII in October 1958, the mood became quite different. There was a move away from conflict in favour of greater understanding; controversy gave way to dialogue; and dialogue became discussion and conversation, so that friendships began to be formed. The shift is unmistakable. The desire for Christian unity was gathering momentum.

It may seem natural to assume that Newman would have little to offer in these matters. That someone who was for long an influence in the Church of England should, upon changing his allegiance, so to speak, be regarded as influential still, seems improbable at best. Yet that assumption is mistaken. Soon after that change, his loyal friend, Edward Pusey, spoke of his conversion as 'perhaps the greatest event which has happened since the Communion of the Churches has been interrupted'. And he gave his reason: 'If anything could open their eyes to what is good in us, or soften in us any wrong prejudices against them, it would be the presence of such an one, nurtured and grown to ripeness in our Church, and now removed to

theirs.'[1] That may seem too optimistic. Nevertheless, the Oxford
Newman Symposium in 1966 declared: ' ... if we wish to find
common elements which, when studied from the differing
Christian standpoints, set the agenda for our mutual growth
towards unity, then we need go no farther back in history than to
Newman'.[2]

Those hostile to Newman will, of course, disagree; they find
him a barrier; but those more sympathetic will regard him as a
bridge. What commends him in particular are his credentials, the
qualities he brought to ecumenical debate. Stephen Dessain
identified four of them: the way he acknowledged what was true
and valuable among Christians in spite of separation; his realism
about the causes of division; his recognition of where Catholicism
fell short; and his desire to offer a complete and balanced account
of Christian truth.[3] These are major attributes, but still the path
could be rocky.

(ii)

One constant personal irritant for Newman as a Catholic were the
rumours that would circulate with tedious regularity about his
disillusionment with the Church he had joined and his imminent
return to Anglicanism. In June 1862, during that gloomy period of
his life after his time in Dublin and his involvement with *The
Rambler*, and before Kingsley's attack provoked his *Apologia*, one
newspaper, *The Globe*, reported the rumour again with great
assurance. In a blistering response, Newman spoke of his unwa-
vering trust in the Catholic Church, his 'unclouded faith in her
creed', and his 'supreme satisfaction in her worship, discipline, and
teaching'. He denied outright that he would ever leave and went

---

1 H. P. Liddon, *The Life of Edward Bouverie Pusey*, 4 vols., (London, 1893 –
   1897), ii, p. 461.
2 Coulson and Allchin (eds.), *The Rediscovery of Newman*, p. xi.
3 See C. S. Dessain, 'Cardinal Newman and Ecumenism', *The Clergy Review* l
   (1965) 119–37, 189–206; see especially 129ff.

on to describe Protestantism as 'the dreariest of possible religions'. The thought of the Anglican service, he stated, made him shiver and the thought of the Thirty-Nine Articles made him shudder. He would be a fool, he said, to return to the Church of England (see *L.D.* xx, pp. 215–16).

These words, of course, pained his estranged Anglican friends, but, as Newman explained to one of them, Charles Crawley, they referred to Protestantism and the Anglican system, not to people, and they were used to force Protestants 'to put out of their minds the hope of my ever coming back to them'. They were 'the deliberately chosen and studied means' of bringing the tiresome rumours to an end (see *L.D.* xx, pp. 234–6). Newman's personal feelings were very different and became evident two years later when he wrote his *Apologia*: ' . . . the Church of England has been the instrument of Providence in conferring great benefits on me' (*Apo.* p. 341 [297]). Old friends realised how deeply he cared for them still. Here was that first credential, the acknowledging of what is true and valuable among others.

And it had always been so. Even in his early Catholic years, he had recoiled from attacks on the Church of England (see *L.D.* xiv, p. 207). He valued what he had received from it. In 1860, for example, he explained to Edgar Estcourt, a former Anglican clergyman who was now Bishop Ullathorne's secretary and treasurer of the Birmingham Diocese, his reasons for opposing the building of a Catholic church in Oxford. He regarded the plan as unnecessarily controversial and likely to weaken the Church of England, when Anglican Oxford was in practice at that time, he pointed out, 'a breakwater against Unitarianism, fanaticism, and infidelity'. And he declared his own debt: 'Catholics did not make us Catholics; Oxford made us Catholics. At present Oxford surely does more good than harm' (*L.D.* xix, p. 352). These words are the more striking because of the way they contrast with some of Manning's. Newman's attempt in his *Letter to Pusey* to offer, as we have seen,[4] a more moderate account of teaching about the Blessed

---

4 See above, p. 63.

Virgin than Faber's and Ward's, had not pleased him. He regarded
Newman's work as 'worldly', a diluting of Catholic doctrine. And
he declared: 'It is the old Anglican, patristic, literary, Oxford tone
transplanted into the Church.'[5] While Newman seemed to value
his past and respectfully and affectionately carry it with him into
his future, so far as he could, Manning seemed suspicious and
hostile. He could be tender towards people, but he had turned his
back utterly on what he had left behind.

Newman's ability to value what was true in the views of other
Christians did not, however, make him blind to difference. It is the
second credential. In his *Apologia*, while he spoke plainly of his
reluctance 'to cause offence to religious Anglicans', he admitted
that he felt bound all the same to confess his 'astonishment that I
had ever imagined [the Church of England] to be a portion of the
Catholic Church'. It reads as a sharp rebuff. He acknowledged its
outstanding qualities as an institution, its wisdom, its political
power, its place in the nation's life, and its witness to and teaching
of religious truth, but he could no longer see it as 'something
sacred'. 'It may be a great creation, though it be not divine, and
this is how I judge of it' (see *Apo*. pp. 339–42 [296–8]). Understanding of the Church, of course, has developed since those days.
Newman did not have at his disposal the nuanced recognition,
supplied by the Second Vatican Council's Decree on Ecumenism,
of a communion between separated Christians which is real
though imperfect (*Unitatis Redintegratio*, no. 3). In his day, the lines
were drawn more starkly.

All the same, while Newman could be forthright about the
difference between the Catholic position and that of others, he was
not blind to Catholic defects, which is the third credential identified by Dessain. In his Journal in 1863 he spoke of his conviction
that 'the Church must be prepared for converts, as well as converts
prepared for the Church' (*A.W.* p. 258). And fourteen years later,
in 1877, he expressed forcibly the difficulty which he saw. 'It is so
ordered on high,' he wrote in his Preface for the third edition of his

---

5 Quoted in Newsome, *The Convert Cardinals*, p. 257.

Lectures on the Prophetical Office, 'that in our day Holy Church should present just that aspect to my countrymen which is most consonant with their ingrained prejudices against her, most unpromising for their conversion' (*V.M.* i, p. xxxvii [23]). This realism about the Church implied recognition of what was true and to be valued among others, as well as what was defective among Catholics. Moreover, it is an example I have tried to follow.

When *The Catholic Faith* first appeared in 1986, it was reviewed on BBC Radio Ulster. The reviewer observed: 'Dr Strange approaches his task with a candour that apologists for other Christian traditions would do well to imitate. Self-criticism in religious writing is like the bitter lemon that brings out the flavour in good fish. So Dr Strange does not hesitate to meet head on nastiness wherever he finds it ... throughout these pages the author is, if anything, prepared to err on the side of ecumenical generosity.' I appreciated then, and do so now, these kind words which, I would add, once more bear witness to Newman's influence. Nevertheless, the reviewer reserved a sting for the tail. 'For all that,' he added, 'a real Catholic heart beats beneath the veneer of benign ecumenism.'[6] I am proud of my Catholic heart, but long to overcome the suspicion suggested by that final phrase. How might it be done? And here the fourth credential comes into play, the desire to offer a complete and balanced account of Christian truth.

Exploring Newman's life and thought has already raised for us a number of issues which sometimes have been seen as controversial. Liberalism in religion pointed to the possible tension between dogma and theology. There were those who saw dogma always as dogmatizing, an assault on the freedom to think which is essential for theology; and there were those who viewed theology as lacking focus or definition. Newman, however, championed dogma when it was threatened, but sought to safeguard freedom for theology when it was not. Then again, papal infallibility was

6 Review by David Livingstone, 'Sunday Sequence', BBC Radio Ulster, 23 March 1986.

feared by some as the gateway to doctrinal tyranny, while it was eulogized by others who tried to extend its boundaries. Newman, as we noticed, placed it in a larger context, seeking to calm fears and clip the wings of extremists. Then there were some who could make no sense of the place of the laity in the Church; for them they were simply 'boys eternal'. Newman, on the other hand, viewed their situation very differently. Driven by his commitment to education, he wanted to equip them for the role they needed to play. On each occasion, he tried to avoid extremes and offer an account on which people could agree and around which they could unite. For us it is not a matter of agreeing with each particular position he took. We may, or we may not. More important is the strategy, an attractive, gentle handling of contentious issues which seeks to clarify misunderstandings so that they may be overcome. Nevertheless, even this strategy is not everything. Something more is needed.

Consider another testing area for ecumenical discussion, Mary, the Mother of the Lord. The Anglican-Roman Catholic International Commission produced its document, *Mary: Grace and Hope in Christ*, in 2004. Newman explored such matters in his *Letter to Pusey* in 1866. Here too, he followed his customary path by trying to moderate extremism, clarify misunderstandings, and present an account on which all could agree. We have already seen the substance of what he had to say,[7] but there is a rarer, more particular lesson to be learnt from that controversy. It touches the very heart of ecumenical discussion and emerges from an awareness of the circumstances that led to it and the conditions in which it took place. It makes an intriguing story.

(iii)

On 12 September 1865 Newman visited Keble in his vicarage at Hursley. The visit had been planned for some time, but at the last moment he almost decided not to go, because he heard that Pusey

---

7 See above, pp. 62–76.

was by chance visiting the same day. The three of them had not met for about twenty years and he felt it might all be too much at last to see both of them together. But then he thought better of it; he felt he was being cowardly; so he turned up unannounced. The visit went well. They talked for four or five hours and had dinner together, something they must have done often in the past in Oriel at high table or with other friends, but, Newman noted later, extraordinary as it may seem to us, it was 'the first and last time in their lives' that they had dined together 'simply by themselves' (*L.D.* xxiv, p. 142; see *L.D.* xxii, pp. 51–3).

The following month news of their meeting became known. It was reported in the press that Pusey and Newman had been reconciled. Pusey was offended and wrote to the editor of the Tractarian newspaper, the *Guardian*, on 9 October to correct the very idea that reconciliation could ever have been called for. 'The deep love between us,' he declared, 'which now dates back for above forty years, has never been in the least overshadowed. His leaving us was one of the deep sorrows of my life; but it involved separation of place, not diminution of affection.'[8] This declaration of his bond with Newman sets the scene for what happened next.

At the time of their meeting, Pusey had become embroiled in a controversy with Manning who had just become the Archbishop of Westminster. Manning, in a public letter to Pusey, had reacted to a popular view which had identified him as one of those Roman Catholics who were, in a phrase of Pusey's, 'in an ecstasy of triumph' over certain troubles within the Church of England. He wanted to set the record straight. His pamphlet, though not unsympathetic, was marked by his characteristic vigour and directness, rejoicing in the workings of the Holy Spirit within the Anglican Church, but unable to 'regard the Church of England as "the great bulwark against infidelity in this land"'.[9] Pusey, challenged, felt called to answer Manning's charges; but he also saw the

---

8 Quoted in Liddon, *Life of Edward Bouverie Pusey*, iv, p. 112.
9 See H. E. Manning, *The Workings of the Holy Spirit in the Church of England: a Letter to the Rev. E.B. Pusey, D.D.*, (London, 1865), pp. 6–7.

exchange as an opportunity to promote the reunion of the Christian Church. He named his reply *An Eirenicon*.[10]

During his conversation with Newman and Keble, Pusey was full of this work and at the time Newman had neither the desire nor the inclination to become involved. In fact he and Pusey had already discussed the matter by letter. Ten months earlier he had remarked, 'Of course I do not see things on your side sufficiently to be able to say that you should not answer [Manning] – but I am tempted to ask, Why should you?' (*L.D.* xxi, p. 315).

One part of Pusey's approach was to draw up a list of Roman excesses in devotion to Mary, such as the views that, while Jesus in fact gained us our salvation out of obedience to his Father, he could have won it out of deference to his Mother,[11] and that, as well as the Christ, it is Mary who is present and received in the eucharist.[12] When his book appeared, reviewers were appalled. R. W. Church, the future Dean of St Paul's and a friend of both Pusey and Newman, expressed his revulsion in *The Times*: ' ... there is something absolutely bewildering, like the imaginations of a sick dream, in this audacious extravagance of dogmatism, unfolding itself inexhaustibly into ever stranger and more startling conclusions.'[13] This revulsion, of course, was the very reaction that Pusey wished to arouse among Catholics, in the hope that they would dismiss the extravagance and so make reconciliation easier and more likely. Newman had no doubt that his plan had misfired.

At first he was silent. He was disappointed, because he felt Pusey had exaggerated. He believed that his unbalanced presentation of Roman practices was only going to make matters worse. Pusey had made no attempt, he pointed out to Keble, 'to soften the impression he leaves on the reader, of the *universality*' of extreme views held by people like Faber. He made such views seem

10 E. B. Pusey, *An Eirenicon in a Letter to the Author of 'The Christian Year'*, (London, 1865).

11 See Pusey, *Eirenicon*, pp. 158–9.

12 See Pusey, *Eirenicon*, pp. 169–72.

13 R. W. Church, 'An Eirenicon', in *Occasional Papers*, (London, 1897), i, p. 354.

common to all. 'The whole tone', he declared, 'is antagonistic' (*L.D.* xxii, pp. 91–2). He finally wrote to Pusey himself at the end of October and admitted his disappointment. He told him: 'An Irenicon smoothes difficulties; I am sure people will think that you increase them' (*L.D.* xxii, p. 90).

Pusey, of course, was pained by Newman's reaction. He did not wish to appear hostile in fact, under the guise of speaking peace. He had tried to illustrate his case by using serious authors and he told Newman, 'I thought, "There it is; if any of it is disowned, it is a gain."'[14] Newman wrote back the following day, 5 November, reassuring Pusey that his intention had not been lost on him, but he feared that most people would miss that point and settle down to the parts they could understand more easily (see *L.D.* xxii, p. 93). He also mentioned that at that time he still had no intention of publishing anything himself, but he promised him that, if he did, it would be in the spirit of an eirencon, in the cause of peace.

They continued to exchange letters, Pusey gently but firmly pressing his case, while Newman replied frankly and directly. Keble feared their relationship might cool. 'I do hope he [Newman] will not waver in his friendship for you,' he remarked to Pusey.[15] The fear was unfounded. At the very time of disagreeing with him, Newman was also writing to Pusey enthusiastically, offering to help with the French translation of his book and advising him to delay its publication so that he could take into account any comments from Manning (see *L.D.* xxii, p. 102), while Pusey wrote wondering whether Newman 'could draw up something which I might put before the English Church, as firm to offer'.[16] They were most cordial disputants.

On 24 November it seems that Newman had still not finally decided to join the debate, but four days later he left for Rednal,

14 Liddon, *Life of Pusey*, iv, pp. 121–3.
15 See Liddon, *Life of Pusey*, iv, p. 125.
16 Pusey to Newman, 13 November 1865; printed in R. D. Middleton, *Newman at Oxford*, (London, 1950), pp. 250–1.

the Oratorians' house in the country outside Birmingham, to prepare his response.

(iv)

Newman was moved to write at last by more than the need to answer Pusey. He also felt keenly the harshness of Rome's dealings with Catholic members of the Association for the Promotion of the Unity of Christendom. Membership had been prohibited the previous year and an appeal by 187 Anglicans had led only to a condemnation of a branch theory of the Church. Such events created the impression that all Catholics were as extreme as Faber and Ward (see *L.D.* xxii, p. 110). Newman wished to qualify that impression. He wanted to answer Pusey without causing him pain (see *L.D.* xxii, p. 112) and he hoped also, as we have seen earlier, that if he confined his remarks to the mariological section, he might supply an alternative to the mariological excesses of writers like Ward and Faber which created such an obstacle for others. That was why he stated in his published *Letter* that he wanted people to know, 'did they come to stand where I stand, what they would, and what they would not, be bound to hold concerning [the Blessed Virgin]' (*Diff.* ii, p. 25).[17]

At Rednal Newman wrote at great speed. He also sent letters to both Keble and Pusey on 8 December, the feast of the Immaculate Conception, so that they knew what he was doing. He stressed to them his wish not to cause pain and his desire to preserve the eirenical spirit (see *L.D.* xxii, pp. 118–19). Pusey replied the next day. The controversy had gathered momentum and he was relieved that Newman was taking part. He noted: 'This discussion is taking too wide a range, for me to wish you to be silent.'[18] And indeed Newman wrote eirenically, true to his conviction that 'Abuse is as great a mistake in controversy, as panegyric in biography' (*L.D.* xxii, p. 211).

17 See above, p. 63.
18 Liddon, *Life of Pusey*, iv, p. 131.

It is not surprising that Newman was able to write so fast. He was on familiar ground, throwing parts of his *Essay on Development* into more popular form and distilling ideas that he had expressed previously in private letters. He explained the difference between Faber and Ward, on the one hand, and himself, on the other, and tried to make clear the distinctions between doctrine and devotion and between intercession and invocation. He also repudiated foreign extravagance as 'a bad dream', 'calculated to prejudice inquirers, to frighten the unlearned, to unsettle consciences, to provoke blasphemy, and to work the loss of souls' (*Diff.* ii, pp. 113–15). His *Letter* was published on 31 January.

After publication, Keble wrote within days, gracious as ever, and Pusey wrote soon afterwards. He too was grateful, especially for Newman's kind words about himself, but all the same he took the opportunity to explain various points which he disputed. And so the controversy continued. Both men received praise and rebuke from their own communions as well as from each other's. Pusey went on to write two further volumes of *Eirenicon*, both addressed as *Letters* to Newman, while Newman eventually continued his reply to Pusey, almost ten years later, when he responded to Gladstone's views about authority and the papacy in his *Letter to the Duke of Norfolk*. Their business remained unfinished.

(v)

The outcome of this exchange may well seem disappointing. It had had so much to commend it. It is, after all, relatively rare for two people who enjoy so close and affectionate a friendship to be locked in public debate, disagreeing sharply, but without acrimony. Moreover, as we have seen, their friendship meant that they were able to discuss their separate positions in private letters as well as by the exchange of their published works. And then the sympathy between them seemed to create the most favourable climate for resolving their disagreement satisfactorily. Yet the progress they made was slight. Indeed, at the end they did not really seem any closer than they had been at the beginning. Why? Two reasons in particular suggest themselves.

First, it may well be that the very understanding of the Church which they employed defeated them from the start. Newman held to the claim of the Roman Catholic Church to be exclusively the Church of Christ, while Pusey worked with the branch theory of the Church with all the complexities and questions which that involves. Again, although both desired reunion, they were prompted to write for different motives. Pusey wanted to answer the charges levelled by Manning, while Newman in addressing Pusey was concerned primarily to make public and establish openly an English disposition to certain Catholic doctrines and devotions which at that time were suffering from an excessive amount of continental colour and influence. In the circumstances, it is hardly surprising that their exchanges were not more fruitful. Were they, therefore, a waste of time? Have they nothing to teach us so many years later? Not necessarily.

One sentence from this controversy has become famous. At the beginning of his public *Letter*, Newman took Pusey to task for calling his book *An Eirenicon*. 'There was one of old time', he remarked, 'who wreathed his sword in myrtle; excuse me – you discharge your olive-branch as if from a catapult' (*Diff.* ii, p. 7). Henry Liddon, Pusey's friend and biographer, acknowledged the turn of phrase, but called it unjust, for it 'cleverly diverted attention from the fact that the sting lay in the obstacles themselves and not in their enumeration'.[19] Church, on the other hand, reviewing Newman's *Letter* in *The Times* on 31 March 1866, agreed wholeheartedly with Newman: 'This is, no doubt, exactly what Dr. Pusey has done.'[20] Such reactions are instructive.

Liddon's meaning is plain enough. In fact Church's was the same. He was arguing that Pusey had no alternative but belligerence. He had given more credit to Rome than most people would have thought possible, and so it was necessary to state the obstacles also,

19 Liddon, *Life of Pusey*, iv, p. 136.
20 Church, *Occasional Papers*, ii, p. 406.

openly and courageously. Church was pleased that Newman had detached himself from these obstacles, the extravagances of the extremists, but he went on to observe, 'it seems to us much more difficult for him to release his cause from complicity with the doctrines which he dislikes and fears'. He then identified the crucial issue, the question 'whether [Newman] or the innovators represent the true character and tendencies of their religious system'.[21]

It is a telling point which cuts to the very heart of ecumenical discussion. It is not answered by making distinctions between doctrine and devotion, invocation and intercession, however necessary and proper those may be in their place. Whether Pusey was inaccurate at times in his exposition or not makes little difference. He had articulated a suspicion and aroused a prejudice, and Church's reaction bore witness to it. All their sympathy and friendship – for Church too was a close friend – could not erase that element of uncertainty. How could it be overcome? The only antidote to suspicion in these circumstances is a more widespread, popular trust. It was possible to believe Newman. But was he really able to speak for the others?

At the very least, therefore, this dispute between Pusey and Newman is a cautionary tale. It illustrates how hard ecumenical discussion can be. The whole episode is a warning that the Agreed Statements on our shelves, on the eucharist, ministry, and authority, on the nature of the Church, Mariology and justification by faith, and on many other subjects besides, will count for little, even combined with love, sympathy and friendship for individuals, unless there also exists among us an unequivocal trust which reaches out widely and is deeply felt. Even then progress may well be slow.

(vi)

Newman's final Anglican sermon, 'The Parting of Friends', was preached on 25 September 1843. It was the sermon heard by the

---

21 Church, *Occasional Papers*, ii, p. 415.

grandfather of the woman who showed me Newman's home in Littlemore on my first visit.[22] His penultimate sermon, however, at least among those which were published, he preached earlier that year at Pentecost. He spoke about the link within the Church between what is personal and what is public. 'We cannot hope for unity of faith,' he remarked, 'if we at our own private will make a faith for ourselves in this our small corner of the earth.' It is not difficult to imagine the pressure he must have been feeling at that time as he wrestled with his situation and struggled to come to a decision. Should he remain an Anglican or turn to Rome? Was the Church of England a faith wedded to its small corner of the earth or was its scope larger? His dilemma is visible between the lines of the text and so it comes as no surprise to hear him describe 'the division of Churches' as 'the corruption of hearts' (*S.D.* p. 133). His distress is evident.

More than twenty years later, debating with Pusey, he was still working to overcome that division. And the manner in which he worked, valuing the good, stating differences, acknowledging defects, and presenting a balanced account of the issues, on the one hand, while, on the other, remaining faithful in love and friendship, sympathy and trust, offer us a path to follow. What better way to heal the corruption of hearts? And if the outcome for Newman in this instance was disappointing, it does not prove he was mistaken. It only shows us that the road ahead is rough. But it remains the right road.

22 See above, p. 79.

8

Strange Providence

(i)

Newman kept a Journal for most of his life. As the years went by, he added to it only occasionally. The entry for 25 June 1869 was the first for more than six months. It began: 'The Providence of God has been wonderful with me all through my life' (*A.W.* p. 267). Various reflections on the ways of providence follow and they include references to the outcome of the three illnesses which he suffered earlier in his life, the first, in boyhood, bringing him to Christianity, the second, as a young Oxford don, leading him to break with liberalism, and the third, as he said, 'in 1833, when I was in Sicily, before the commencement of the Oxford Movement' (*A.W.* p. 268).

This view of his experience in Sicily as providential had been fixed in his mind from the start. He began his account of it in August 1834 with the words, 'I seem to see, and I saw, a strange providence in it' (*A.W.* p. 121). Newman, like most of his contemporaries, had a keen sense of providence. He was to describe it years later as 'nearly the only doctrine held with a real assent by the mass of religious Englishmen' (*G.A.* p. 57 [44]). In any case no student of his life and work could doubt its importance for him. We have seen already how he described the Church of England as 'the instrument of Providence' in conferring benefits on him (*Apo.* p. 341 [297]).[1] And his return to Sicily without his friends in 1833 stood out in his mind as a further powerful example of providence at work in his life. But the idea of providence can cause bewilderment today.

---

1 See above, p. 97.

It is commonly understood simply as God's plan for us. Good luck or a happy coincidence we sometimes describe as providential. But that may lead to seeing it as God intervening, imposing something on our lives which changes the natural course of events. We have obvious difficulties with such a notion, God as the grand chess-master in the sky, moving us about like pawns on the board. If divine providence refers to God's plan, it needs also to refer to something more. So how is this doctrine to be understood? Newman's experience in Sicily seems to me to offer clues. It certainly helped me shape the account I gave in *Living Catholicism*, where I explained it not only as God's plan for us, but as involving also God's presence; and plan and presence, if they are to become providential, require of us perception as well.[2] We need to look more closely at what happened to Newman. And it will help us get to know him better.

(ii)

He spoke of his solitary return to Sicily as 'a strange providence' (*A.W.* p. 121). The description repays attention. The adjective can have various meanings. What is strange can be foreign, alien, hostile. Again, as bearers of the name, victims of countless puns and unoriginal jokes, know to their cost, it can be used as a synonym for what is odd or peculiar. And it can also mean something which causes surprise, amazement, wonder. In that sense, Lord Byron called truth 'stranger than fiction',[3] and in the same sense, I suggest, Newman found his Sicilian adventure strange. The ways of providence took him by surprise, amazed him, caused him to wonder. Remember what had happened.

After the tutorial dispute with Provost Hawkins at Oriel, Newman had been deprived of pupils and so he was free to take a Mediterranean voyage with his friend, Hurrell Froude, and Hurrell's father, who was the Archdeacon of Totnes. During it, as

---

2 See Strange, *Living Catholicism*, pp. 73–8.
3 Lord Byron, *Don Juan*, canto xiv, st. 101.

arranged, they visited Sicily and from there went on to Rome. But then Newman had a fresh idea. He had found Sicily enchanting. He longed to see it again. So, while his friends went back to England through France, he, regardless of them and contrary to plan, decided to retrace his steps. After a while, however, he became dangerously unwell, probably with typhoid fever. He came to see his own behaviour as an example of the very wilfulness against which he had preached in Oxford the day before setting off on this holiday. At the same time, he felt with growing confidence a sense of vocation in his returning to England, because he was convinced that God had a work for him to do.

What account can be given of the ways of providence in this experience? The plans of providence are commonly recognised only with hindsight. It might be asked, what was God planning for Newman in Sicily? Was it the stimulus to return to England on fire with a sense of mission? That might seem the natural answer. But Newman himself saw in this second, unplanned visit to the island an act of wilfulness. Did God sow the wilful seed? That would make matters more complicated. We must proceed with care. One of the most confusing and least helpful features in the discussion of providence is the tendency to identify every aspect of what takes place as some particular divine intervention. That would lead people into supposing, for example, that it was God who prompted Newman to leave his friends and return wilfully to Sicily so that there in a lonely place he could strike him down with a dangerous illness and thereby reform his life and reveal to him his mission. We have to unravel the threads. We can begin with Newman's idea of wilfulness.

(iii)

In his memoir, written in 1834, Newman saw the strange providence of his illness as a judgement and a punishment. It was a judgement on him, he believed, because he felt he had received the eucharist unworthily, owing to the resentment he had still borne Edward Hawkins, the Provost of Oriel, over the tutorial dispute. It was a punishment, he said, 'for my wilfulness in going to Sicily by myself' (*A.W.* p. 121). He had reported his awareness of his wilfulness already. It occurred in his earliest written account of his experience, the letter he sent to his friend, Henry Wilberforce, a week after his return. He explained that he came to feel God fighting with him. He went on:

> I came to think that there was some wilfulness in my coming to Sicily, as I did ... And then I felt more than I had done the wilfulness of my character generally ... And then I recollected that the very day before I left Oxford, I had preached a University Sermon against wilfulness, so that I seemed to have been predicting my own condemnation. (*L.D.* iv, p. 8)

This reference to his sermon, 'Wilfulness, the Sin of Saul', is intriguing (see *U.S.* pp. 156–75). It is not as straightforward as it may seem. In the sermon wilfulness is always a sin, while Newman told Wilberforce that, although he became aware of having sinned, he had been comforted in his illness by a sense of not having brought the situation on himself by going against advice and by the phrase that had come back to him and which he had repeated often, 'I have not sinned against the light'. So Newman's allusion to his wilfulness may be explained more naturally as characteristic of someone whose view of himself is at a low ebb. He may not have sinned gravely, but he had been stubborn. His return to Sicily seemed to have lacked consideration for his friends. As he observed: ' ... though no one had advised me against it, yet I fancied I ought to have discovered they thought it an over-venturous thing' (*L.D.* iv, p. 8). Certainly it was marked by his determination to do what he wanted to do. These features of his visit match well his description of wilfulness in the sermon as 'the unaccountable desire of acting short of simple obedience to God's will, a repugnance of unreserved self-surrender and submission to Him' (*U.S.* p. 161). Newman's return to Sicily may not have involved serious sin; he was not sinning against the light; but his behaviour was flawed by mixed motives. And then he fell ill.

To understand the working of providence as Newman perceived it in the light of his Sicilian visit, it is essential to remember
that there was no trace of his wrestling with God, his brooding on
his failings, or his dark judgement of himself, until the illness
struck. Here was the strange providence, the cause of surprise and
wonder. His perilous condition brought about a revelation of
divine presence. His declining fortunes in Oxford, his resentment
at the Provost, the general state of fatigue which had led him to
join the Froudes for this holiday, may all have combined, even in
him whose sense of God's presence was so vivid, to dull his
awareness of that presence. The illness revived it.

It was a crisis whose effects were spiritual as well as physical.
Suddenly he saw the obstacles which had troubled him since
leaving the Froudes in Rome – presumably the difficulties and
delays which had beset his return to the island – as signs of God
fighting against him. He recognised the poor manner of his
behaviour over the tutorial dispute and the way his resentment of
the Provost had, as he judged it, made his reception of the
eucharist unworthy. And in his very journey to Sicily he discovered a particular example of the general wilfulness which, he
concluded, marred his character. He indulged his own will too
much. He seemed at least to resemble Saul who had 'preferred his
own way to that which God had determined' (*U.S.* p. 164). Here
there was lacking that unreserved self-surrender and submission to
the divine will that he had so urged upon others. Nevertheless, in
spite of these hazards, his resistance to God and his wilfulness, he
felt comforted even in the depths of his sickness. He was comforted, he told Wilberforce, because he had not gone against any
advice which he had actually received and because of his sense that
he had not 'sinned against the light'. And then, he added, 'I
thought I would try to obey God's will as far as I could' (*L.D.* iv,
p. 8). What a strange providence indeed to have been so preserved
from serious sin and then enlightened by grave illness. On his way
home on 16 June, becalmed at sea, Newman poured his feelings
into three brief stanzas.

For many years congregations have delighted in singing 'Lead,

Kindly Light', largely oblivious of its origins (*V.V.* pp. 156–7). To know its source, the relief and gratitude which inspired it, is to recognise instantly its intense personal character for Newman and to understand why he could not bear to hear it sung in his own Oratory in Birmingham. It captured poignantly his experience of the kindly light which had guided him through darkness when he was far from home: one step was enough; it acknowledged the wilfulness which once had loved to see and choose its own path, but now no longer; it professed hope in the power that would continue to guide him over rough countryside of every kind – moor and fen, crag and torrent – till the night was gone and there remained only angel faces and perfect love.

These reflections in Newman's letter to Wilberforce, in his memoir, and in his poem followed very closely upon the experience itself. They are too immediate for a clear view of this strange providence to emerge. His understanding of that can be seen better by complementing his account with his observations about providence in later years. Sicily was never mentioned, but its influence is unmistakable.

(iv)

Consider first the sermon 'Divine Calls', which Newman preached on 27 October 1839 (see *P.S.* viii, pp. 17–32). He took as his text a verse from the first Book of Samuel: 'And the Lord came, and stood, and called as at other times, Samuel, Samuel. Then Samuel answered, "Speak; for Thy servant heareth"' (1 Sam. 3:10). He drew from it the lesson of prompt obedience to the call and added a number of other examples, David, Paul and various apostles, on the one hand, the rich young man and various waverers, on the other, all of whom, by their acceptance or refusal, illustrated the same lesson. The characteristic of divine calls, he concluded, was 'to require instant obedience' (*P.S.* viii, p. 22). Remembering Sicily, we may hear these words as a reproach to that wilfulness which acts 'short of simple obedience to God's will' (*U.S.* p. 161). And he went on at once in the sermon to notice that divine calls 'call us we know not to what; [they] call us on in darkness' (*P.S.* viii, p. 22), which seems to echo his poem: 'The night is dark, and I am far from home – / Lead Thou me on!' (*V.V.* p. 156).

Next, the sermon reflects on the many calls that people receive throughout their lives, from sin to repentance, from grace to grace, from holiness to holiness. People who live religiously, Newman explained, 'have from time to time truths they did not know before, or had no need to consider, brought before them forcibly: truths which involve duties, which are in fact precepts, and claim obedience'. These are occasions when Christ is calling them, they are particular moments, and yet in themselves they are unexceptional. He observed: 'There is nothing miraculous or extraordinary in His dealings with us. He works through our natural faculties and circumstances of life.' And this divine action, carried out in everyday ways, Newman spoke of as providential: 'Still what happens to us in providence is in all essential respects what His voice was to those whom He addressed when on earth' (*P.S.* viii, p. 24). How well this description captures the pattern of that strange providence which overtook Newman in Sicily: a lesson learnt afresh about obedience to God's will through the suffering of an ordinary, although serious, illness.

The impression that his experience in Sicily is an implicit influence is reinforced when Newman went on to remind his congregation about the way in which these calls occur. They are commonly sudden and unexpected. He mentioned how a letter, a message, or a person can provide a trial which, 'if met religiously', can be the means of bringing someone to a high state of knowledge and holiness. An unexpected illness would have been as apt an example. Crises force us to take stock. He stressed further that he was not speaking of cases in which people change their whole lives or reverse their opinions and conduct. Outwardly they remain much as they were, just like himself after Sicily, we may add; but inwardly they have got into 'a new world of thought' and they measure things and persons 'by a different rule', again, just as he had done (*P.S.* viii, pp. 25–6).

There is no question of claiming that this sermon was conceived intentionally as a commentary on his illness in Sicily, but even what a person forgets can influence his imagination, and the view of providence that he presented here dovetails noticeably with that experience. It would be more surprising if it did not. His illness was providential. But there was more to the providence than that event alone. Perhaps the key remark about these calls is his observation, 'We are slow to master the great truth, that Christ is, as it were, walking among us, and by His hand, or eye, or voice, bidding us follow Him' (*P.S.* viii, p. 24). Providence is at work among us not merely as a plan, but also through presence. The ordinary outward event is recognised as providential when the divine presence is perceived within. There are two layers and they combine.

(v)

Two years later, in 1841, Newman turned again to the question of providence when he reviewed Henry Hart Milman's *History of Christianity*. If the emphasis in the sermon could be said to favour the event or plan within which the presence is discerned, the review lays stress rather on the presence which is at work within the plan. At first it might not seem so. Newman stated: 'Now it has ever been a firm article of Christian faith, that [God's] Providence is in fact not general merely, but is, on the contrary, thus particular and personal'. The reference to the particular and personal may seem to suggest intervention, the intrusive outward event. But Newman at once continued: '. . . as there is a particular Providence, so of necessity that Providence is secretly concurring and co-operating with that system which meets the eye, and which is commonly recognized among men as existing.' Providence operates within the ordinary. He then laid down what he called 'the one great rule' for God's relationship with the human race and creation: 'the visible world is the instrument, yet the veil of the world invisible, – the veil, yet still partially the symbol and index: so that all that exists or happens visibly, conceals and yet suggests, and above all subserves, a system of persons, facts, and events beyond itself' (*Ess.* ii, p. 192). We hear the chord of romantic Platonism being firmly struck, the conviction that, as symbols participate in the reality which they symbolise, so the visible world veils a world unseen.[4] Newman declared: 'All that is seen, – the world, the Bible, the Church, the civil polity, and man himself, – are types, and in their degree and place, representatives and organs of an unseen world, truer and higher than themselves.' He allowed that there was a distinction to be drawn: some things may seem to be more obviously supernatural or symbolical, while others seem to be complete in themselves, or may even seem opposed to the unseen system which in fact they serve and support (see *Ess.* ii, p. 193). But all that is and so much that occurs, whether evident or not, is the veil and vehicle of the divine presence.

'When Providence would make a Revelation,' Newman observed, 'He [God] does not begin anew, but uses the existing system': priests give us his blessing, the elements of this world are used to consecrate us and give us life, divine order follows a natural form. Even miracles are worked, he remarked, 'without super-seding the ordinary course of things'. He gave as examples the increase of Jacob's flocks and descendants and their deliverance from Egypt, and concluded: 'But still the operation of ordinary causes, the influence of political arrangements, and what is called the march of events, are seen in such providences as truly, and can be pointed out as convincingly, as if an Angel or a pillar of a cloud were not with them' (*Ess.* ii, p 194). The pre-critical colouring of these observations makes their content all the more telling. And, although unmentioned, his experience in Sicily is a natural illus-tration of this teaching. These words express so well what had happened to him. Everything that took place, leading up to his illness as well as the illness itself, is entirely explicable by natural causes; yet it brought about a revelation of God's presence which flooded his being, convinced him of his recovery, and instilled in him a sense of mission. As he was to tell Henry Wilberforce: 'I

---

4 See above, p. 38; see also Prickett, *Romanticism and Religion*, pp. 114–19.

could not help saying, I must act as if I were to die, but I think God has work for me yet' (*L.D.* iv, p. 8). Here, once again, we are led to the conclusion that in providence plan and presence combine, outward event and inward reality are one.

So far, perhaps, so good. We can set aside the shallow notion that providence is God acting in an intrusive, manipulative way. The events which are providential have natural causes. We have seen, moreover, that God is always present and that it is the inner reality of his abiding presence which makes what takes place providential. But now we may discover a fresh difficulty. If God is always present, in what sense is providence particular? This emphasis on his abiding presence seems to empty the teaching on providence of any distinctive content. Something further needs to be said. We must investigate more deeply. We can do so by turning to a slightly earlier sermon, preached in 1835 and called 'A Particular Providence as revealed in the Gospel' (*P.S.* iii, pp. 114–27).

(vi)

Drawing on a wide range of biblical examples, from Balaam to Judas, Newman developed this theme. God is good and everyone is in his presence. All the same, crises occur as that presence is neglected or forgotten. This, he said, 'is often the state in which persons find themselves on falling into trouble. The world fails them, and they despair, because they do not realize to themselves the loving-kindness and the presence of God' (*P.S.* iii, p. 117). Their fortunes begin to change when they rediscover that presence. The rediscovery makes it seem like a new truth and it is that rediscovery which is providential. 'Some especial Providence,' he noted, 'amid their affliction, runs right into their heart, and brings it close home to them, in a way they had never experienced before, that God sees them.' This surprise brings delight and can even sweep them to the opposite extreme, making them suppose that they are loved more than others. They are mistaken. There is a 'particular Providence over all' (*P.S.* iii, p. 118). Each and all are loved by God individually. In a passage, memorable for me because of the impression it made on me when I first read it, Newman evoked this humbling and awe-inspiring truth:

> God beholds thee individually, whoever thou art. He 'calls thee by thy name.' He sees thee, and understands thee, as He made thee. He knows what is in thee, all thy own peculiar feelings and thoughts, thy dispositions and likings, thy strength and thy weakness. He views thee in thy day of rejoicing, and thy day of sorrow. He sympathizes in thy hopes and thy temptations. He interests Himself in all thy anxieties and remembrances, all the risings and fallings of thy spirit.

There is much more and at its core we find the declaration, 'Thou dost not love thyself better than He loves thee' (*P.S.* iii, pp. 124–5).[5] What more could we ask?

The account of providence which emerges in these writings teaches that it operates on three levels, or is composed of three dimensions. First of all, God is indeed at work. He is acting in the particular and personal way which is appropriate to each individual. Providence, for Newman, is not just a turn of phrase. He believed that God has a plan which is being fulfilled. Its action is not interference. It is a part of the ordinariness of everyday life, its laws, its sequence of cause and effect. Secondly, the inner reality of this plan is God's abiding presence within all his creation. Living in that presence and responding to that plan, whether by acceptance or refusal, is the very nature of the human condition. But the particular feature which makes a situation providential is a third element, the recognition by the individual of the divine presence within the events which are taking place. What we designate as providential are those moments or occasions when we become aware of God's will for us. They are privileged perceptions of his abiding presence.

5 See above, p. 9.

Once again, we may detect Newman's experience in Sicily behind this teaching because it illustrates it so well. His illness was a strange providence. Although intelligible in natural terms, Newman saw it nonetheless as a particular event through which he came to recognise afresh God's presence to himself and thereby came also to know his will. Plan, presence, and perception coincided.

This teaching has value still. Of course, it may disappoint those who think simplistically of providence as divine intervention. They may feel bewildered or become angry when life is hard; they want God to intervene and solve their difficulties. Divine power, however, is not like that, a merely superhuman power; and God's providence, as Newman implied, is not an occasional, intrusive, manipulative presence, but one that remains with us both in tragedy and joy. Moments which we recognise as providential are like sacraments of God's love; they are the times when we perceive more clearly God's plan for us and his love as an abiding and present reality.[6]

(vii)

Newman's experience in Sicily was so powerful it seems natural to wonder how long its impact endured.

In the *Apologia*, Newman described his return to England in nervous, staccato sentences (*Apo.* p. 35 [43]). Father Henry Tristram, who first edited Newman's autobiographical papers at the Birmingham Oratory, long after Newman had died, noted how they conjured up, even after thirty years, the 'mental tension under which he laboured' (*A.W.* p. 119). Yet over the page, beginning a new section, Newman commented disarmingly, 'I soon relapsed into the every-day life I had hitherto led' (*Apo.* p. 36 [44]). The intensity of the moment was not maintained; that was hardly to be expected. Nevertheless, the effect did endure.

Newman acknowledged that he was 'in all things the same,

---

6 See Strange, *Living Catholicism*, pp. 77–8; 46–9.

except that a new object was given me' (*Apo.* p. 36 [44]). He was
referring to his sense of a new mission and the part he was to play
in the Oxford Movement. That, too, passed in time. But what
seems never to have passed, however much the experience may
have faded, was his renewed sense of the intimate, personal presence of God. What had impressed him in his youth and perhaps
become jaded by bereavement, disappointment, and fatigue, was
restored in Sicily and never left him. Its effect can be detected in a
meditation which was published only after his death. It speaks of
his part in God's plan, and it can speak also to us:

> I am created to do something or to be something for which
> no one else is created; I have a place in God's counsels, in
> God's world, which no one else has; whether I be rich or
> poor, despised or esteemed by man, God knows me and calls
> me by name.
>
> God has created me to do Him some definite service; He
> has committed some work to me which He has not com-
> mitted to another. I have my mission – I never may know it
> in this life, but I shall be told it in the next. Somehow I am
> necessary for His purposes, as necessary in my place as an
> Archangel in his – . . . I have a part in this great work; I am a
> link in a chain, a bond of connexion between persons. He
> has not created me for naught. I shall do good, I shall do His
> work; I shall be an angel of peace, a preacher of truth in my
> own place, while not intending it, if I do but keep His
> commandments and serve Him in my calling.
>
> Therefore I will trust Him. Whatever, wherever I am, I
> can never be thrown away. If I am in sickness, my sickness
> may serve Him; in perplexity, my perplexity may serve Him;
> if I am in sorrow, my sorrow may serve Him. My sickness, or
> perplexity, or sorrow may be necessary causes of some great
> end, which is quite beyond us. He does nothing in vain; He
> may prolong my life, He may shorten it; He knows what He
> is about. He may take away my friends, He may throw me
> among strangers, He may make me feel desolate, make my

spirits sink, hide the future from me – still He knows what
He is about...

I ask not to see – I ask not to know – I ask simply to be
used. (*M.D.* pp. 399–402)

A sense of the divine presence, of purpose and plan, breathes
through this passage. Its prayerful conclusion, 'not to see', but 'to
be used', echoes his poem, 'The Pillar of the Cloud', which he
composed when becalmed, and marks it as a fruit of that strange
providence which overcame him on his Sicilian journey.

9

Preaching a Living Faith

(i)

Newman landed in England after his Mediterranean journey on 8 July 1833. He was back in Oxford the following evening and six days later, 14 July, John Keble preached the Assize Sermon which expressed alarm at what he saw as government intrusion into the rights of the Church of England. Newman always regarded it as the start of the Oxford Movement. There was a meeting soon afterwards to consider the issues which Keble had raised, but Newman was not there. In any case, as we know, he was impatient with such gatherings. In his view, 'Living movements do not come out of committees,' (*Apo.* p. 39 [46]). Soon he had begun the series of short pamphlets which gave the Movement its other name, Tractarian. But even they were not the main source of his influence at that time. He exercised that from the pulpit in the University Church.

Imagine, therefore, that it is about five minutes to four one Sunday afternoon in Oxford in the late 1830s. You are an undergraduate and, as you usually do, you are walking briskly with a group of your friends across Broad Street, down the Turl, and into Radcliffe Square, anxious to reach the University Church by four o'clock. Your College has moved the hour of its evening meal so that it clashes with the service in an attempt to dissuade you and your friends from going to St Mary's at that time, but that manoeuvre has, if anything, only fuelled your enthusiasm to attend. You reach the church and take your place in one of the pews. You try to pray, but feel distracted, as you wait for the preacher to arrive. You are waiting for John Henry Newman.

In old age you will look back on those Sunday afternoons as golden memories. Your thoughts may echo Matthew Arnold's:

> Forty years ago, when I was an undergraduate at Oxford, voices were in the air there which haunt my memory still. Happy the man who in that susceptible season of youth hears such voices! they are a possession to him for ever ... the name of Cardinal Newman is a great name to the imagination still, his genius and his style are still things of power. But he is over eighty years old ... Forty years ago, he was in the very prime of life; he was close at hand to us at Oxford; he was preaching in St. Mary's pulpit every Sunday; he seemed about to transform and to renew what was for us the most national and natural institution in the world, the Church of England. Who could resist the charm of that spiritual apparition, gliding in the dim afternoon light through the aisles of St. Mary's, rising into the pulpit, and then, in the most entrancing of voices, breaking the silence with words and thoughts which were a religious music – sweet, subtle, mournful? I seem to hear him still ...[1]

What was it that Arnold would have heard? What would you have heard? According to Stephen Dessain, it was a balanced exposition of the Christian Gospel as revealed religion, the cause which gave Newman's life its unity.[2] So those who listened in St Mary's each Sunday would have heard teaching on the Three Persons in the one God, on the incarnation, death, and resurrection of Jesus, on salvation, on the indwelling of the Holy Spirit, on the Church, on the sacraments, on holiness, on sin and forgiveness, and on much else besides. It is not possible, of course, to present everything here, but let me try to give the flavour at least of what you and those who went with you to St Mary's during those momentous

---

1 Matthew Arnold, 'Emerson', in R. H. Super (ed.), *Philistinism in England and America*, (University of Michigan Press, 1974), p. 165.
2 See Dessain, *John Henry Newman*, p. xii; see above, p. 33.

years would have heard by presenting some aspects of his account of faith.

This subject, of course, preoccupied Newman on many occasions, notably in his formal *Oxford University Sermons*, in his *Grammar of Assent*, and in the various papers he wrote to hammer out his thought over the years. That material has created a minor industry for philosophers of religion, but I am not planning to add to it unduly here. My concern is more with Newman's pastoral sermons, those sermons where, as Owen Chadwick once remarked, the Oxford Movement's best writing was 'enshrined'.[3] My choice is not arbitrary. Nevertheless, to set the scene, I am going to begin elsewhere.

(ii)

Towards the end of *A Grammar of Assent* we find one of those phrases which does more than state Newman's point of view; it helps to define him as a person. ' . . . if I am asked to convert others by [a smart syllogism],' he declared, 'I say plainly I do not care to overcome their reason without touching their hearts' (*G.A.* p. 425 [273]). I have mentioned it before.[4] Newman wanted always to speak to the heart. It became his motto as a Cardinal, 'Heart speaks to heart – *Cor ad cor loquitur'*. And yet, when we consider his preaching, this statement may at first seem inconsistent.

When Newman preached at St Mary's, he tended to avoid direct controversy, but he was also offering in his account of the Gospel a clear alternative to the viewpoints proposed by his evangelical and liberal contemporaries. They too, however, as he admitted, appealed to the heart. His sermon, 'Self-Contemplation', preached in 1835, referred to evangelical impatience with dogma, which he, of course, championed; his disapproval is unsurprising. But then he went on to mock its insistence on 'a certain state of heart': 'they lay it down as self-evident, that the main purpose of revealed doctrine

---

3 Chadwick, *The Mind of the Oxford Movement*, p. 42; see above, p. 7.
4 See above, pp. 7, 30.

is to affect the heart', so that what does not affect it may safely be rejected or dismissed as relatively unimportant (see *P.S.* ii, pp. 166–8). But wasn't he intent on touching hearts as well? And at the end of the previous year he had preached on 'The Gospel, a Trust Committed to us'. Here he had the liberals in view, those he called 'the reasoners of this age'. He argued that they failed to unfold the mysteries of the Gospel and concentrated instead on analysis, considering creeds merely as 'fetters on souls'. At the same time, however, for them too, 'the great end of the Gospel is the union of hearts in the love of Christ and of each other' (see *P.S.* ii, pp. 259–61). Once more there is this emphasis on the heart. Again, wasn't that his own preoccupation? So was Newman being inconsistent? We need to look more closely.

What he criticised was the view, shared by evangelical and liberal alike, that a doctrine's effect on the heart was the primary test of its significance. Newman's religion of the heart was never a religion of the heart in that sense. He preached a revealed religion and the heart had its place, not as a criterion of significance, but so that what was revealed could be recognised as real by those who heard him, and come alive for them. He wanted to engage the heart, to kindle in people a living faith, that sensitivity to mystery which he once described as 'colourless, like air or water; it is but the medium through which the soul sees Christ; and the soul as little really rests upon it and contemplates it, as the eye can see the air' (*Jfc.* p. 336). Sitting in St Mary's Sunday after Sunday you would have learnt much about this response to revelation, about the nature of a life lived by faith.

(iii)

One of Newman's earliest sermons was called 'Religious Faith Rational', and he preached it on 24 May 1829 (see *P.S.* i, pp. 190–202). What makes it interesting is the way he was already adopting at that time the approach that was to become so characteristic of him later, eschewing theory and settling for empirical observation.

In particular, he emphasised that believing and trusting are inevitable.

He was dismissive of the idea that faith and trust are confined to religion: 'we are acting on trust every hour of our lives,' he remarked. He gave the examples of our memory and our powers of reasoning. 'And what I wish you particularly to observe,' he went on, 'is, that we continually trust our memory and our reasoning powers in this way, though *they often deceive us.*' That is a very typical Newman touch. If in daily life our continued trust in our memory and reason, despite errors, does not make us irrational or credulous, then neither should it do so in religion, for 'When faith is said to be a religious principle, it is (I repeat) the things believed, not the act of believing them, which is peculiar to religion' (*P.S.* i, pp. 191, 192). To believe, to trust, is not only possible for human beings; it is unavoidable.

Next he took the argument a stage further. Remarking that reliance on memory or reasoning powers might be seen as no more than trust in ourselves, he went on to illustrate that reliance on another, on testimony, which is integral to religious faith, is an everyday experience as well. We acknowledge the existence of towns we have never seen and, writing, of course, long before satellite photography, he referred to the way that the British accept that they live on an island, though they have never toured the coastline. We are convinced, he declared, by 'the *report of others*'. And he commented that this faith in testimony is called irrational only 'when religion is concerned'. And he concluded that Scripture 'only bids us act in respect to a future life, as we are every day acting at present' (*P.S.* i, p. 195). We are guided by faith.

One reason for the interest in this sermon is the way it anticipates his approach in *A Grammar of Assent* which he published 41 years later in 1870. There too Newman insisted on the human constitution as a principle and starting-point: 'If I may not assume that I exist, and in a particular way, that is, with a particular mental constitution, I have nothing to speculate about, and had better leave speculation alone' (*G.A.* p. 347 [224]). The example that Great Britain is an island also finds a place in the argument (see

G.A. pp. 294–6 [191–2]), but it is worth noting that Newman's misgiving about the other arguments has hardened. His view that 'it may be said . . . that to trust our senses and reason is in fact nothing more than to trust ourselves' (*P.S.* i, p. 193), has become a 'reluctance to speak of our trusting memory or reason, except indeed by a figure of speech'. Why? 'It seems to me unphiloso-phical,' he explained, 'to speak of trusting ourselves. We are what we are, and we use, not trust our faculties' (*G.A.* p. 61 [46]). In other words, his later, more explicit adherence to the principle of working from the human constitution had revealed the weakness or inappropriateness of those particular illustrations. It had not, however, affected the conclusion that human beings, whether religious or not, necessarily live by faith.

In his 1829 sermon, Newman introduced a further dimension, namely the reason for trusting in God. Belief is not only something natural to human beings and based on testimony, which in this particular case meant the witness of others that sacred scripture comes from God. Newman declared: 'We obey God primarily because we actually feel His presence in our consciences bidding us obey Him' (*P.S.* i, p. 200). The authority of the Bible derives from God, perceived through conscience. At this early date, Newman was already placing specific emphasis on the role of conscience. He was to write about it at length in the *Grammar* (see *G.A.* pp. 105–18 [73–81]) and to preach on it with memorable power and beauty in Dublin on the Fourth Sunday of Advent in 1856 (see *O.S.* pp. 64–6, 74), but it was a prominent theme in his *Parochial Sermons* as well. You would have heard him mentioning it on various occasions, as you sat listening each week. There was a sermon he called 'Faith without Sight', which he preached on St Thomas's Day, 21 December 1834. In fact, it was the forerunner of the Dublin sermon.

In a compact passage, Newman made three closely-linked points. First, he identified those who are religious as those who are attentive to 'the rule of conscience'. Conscience, he explained, is born with them, but not devised by them. It is distinct. And the religious person 'feels bound in duty to submit' to it. Secondly,

therefore, conscience points a person beyond himself: it 'immediately directs his thoughts to some Being exterior to himself, who
gave it, and who evidently is superior to him'. It follows from that
sense of being duty-bound to submit, 'for a law implies a lawgiver,
and a command implies a superior'. And thirdly, there is a fine
interweaving of what is external and what is interior. 'Thus',
Newman went on,

> a man is at once thrown out of himself [*external*], by the very
> Voice which speaks within him [*interior*]; and while he rules
> his heart and conduct by his inward sense of right and wrong,
> not by the maxims of the external world [*interior*], still that
> inward sense does not allow him to rest in himself, but sends
> him forth again from home to seek abroad for Him who has
> put His word in him [*external*] . . . He looks out of himself for
> the Living Word to which he may attribute what has echoed
> in his heart [*external and interior*]. (*P.S.* ii, p. 18)

To live by faith is to live in obedience to conscience. The voice of
conscience alerts the believer to the authority on which that faith
rests.

There is similar teaching in another sermon, 'Faith without
Demonstration', which Newman first preached on 21 May 1837.
There too he argued against those who sought rational proof for
belief. He maintained that we commonly trust the opinions of
others, for example, in legal matters, without becoming experts
ourselves. We rely on authority. So it is not unreasonable to do the
same in religion. And to the objection that the law of the land is
not improbable or difficult, while, for instance, the Catholic
teaching on the Trinity is mysterious and unlikely, Newman
replied that that is just what we should expect: 'I do not say that it
is true, *because* it is mysterious; but if it *be* true, it cannot help being
mysterious' (*P.S.* vi, p. 333). And he pursued the point further. In
the end, however, he acknowledged that the Being of God cannot
be proved. There may be much to impress us, to strengthen us in
faith, to encourage devotion, but the unbeliever will not be moved

to faith by strict, formal evidence. It does not have that power. Instead, Newman urged, we must learn to walk by faith, and he returned to the role of conscience:

> There is a voice within us, which assures us that there is something higher than earth. We cannot analyze, define, contemplate what it is that thus whispers to us. It has no shape or material form. There is that in our hearts which prompts us to religion, and which condemns and chastises sin. And this yearning of our nature is met and sustained, it finds an object to rest upon, when it hears of the existence of an All-powerful, All-gracious Creator. It incites us to a noble faith in what we cannot see. (*P.S.* vi, pp. 339–40).

In these sermons, therefore, Newman was arguing for the reasonableness of faith, not by supplying some incontrovertible logical proof, but by pointing to the trust that is common among human beings and our reliance on authority. At the same time, he indicated the authority upon which religious faith rests, by appealing to the way conscience alerts us to God's existence and the reality of his presence. That may be its basis. What, however, is its reality? In what does religious faith consist?

(iv)

For Newman an essential part of the answer to that question identified faith with obedience. He preached on that topic in 1830 and declared: 'To believe is to look beyond this world to God, and to obey is to look beyond this world to God, to believe is of the heart, and to obey is of the heart; to believe is not a solitary act, . . . and to obey is not a solitary act . . .' He acknowledged that faith and obedience stand for different ideas in our minds, but asserted that in fact they are 'but one thing viewed differently' (*P.S.* iii, pp. 80–1). The relationship between faith and obedience was a regular theme in his sermons (see *P.S.* viii, pp. 201–16; *P.S.* v, pp. 166, 183–4), but these themes are woven together in a way that rewards particular study in his sermon, 'Saving Knowledge'. It was composed early in 1835, as the Oxford Movement, then barely eighteen months old, was beginning to gather momentum. It is set down as a sermon for Easter Monday.

The 'saving knowledge' of the title is the knowledge of God, revealed in the flesh, Jesus Christ, the incarnate Lord. But if the knowledge of God is eternal life, how are we to know that we know him? That is the question Newman raised. What assurance do we have that we are not in a dream or mistaken? Some Christians, he observed, believed their faith to carry with it its own evidence. He was not convinced so easily. He quoted St John: 'Hereby do we know that we love Him, if we keep His commandments' (1 John 2:3), and commented: 'Obedience is the test of Faith.' These two, faith and obedience, he saw as 'the whole duty and work of the Christian' (P.S. ii, p. 153).

Then he referred to the kind of teaching we were noticing earlier which was dismissive of doctrine and regarded doing good 'as a mere cold and formal morality', while it insisted instead on 'a spiritual state of heart' (*P.S.* ii, p. 154). But Newman insisted on faith and obedience, obedience as evidence of faith. He had in mind general obedience, not just one good quality or another. There is some good in everyone. But the habit of obedience is necessary. 'The more we *do*, the more shall we trust in Christ' (*P.S.* ii, p. 160). Obedience leads to faith and then becomes its fruit and guarantee.

This insistence on obedience may be rare nowadays. Some years ago in Oxford, I planned to preach on it and called in at a local bookshop which was well stocked with theology. 'Have you got anything on obedience?' I asked. With a smile I was told, 'Nobody's writing about obedience these days.' Yet, for the Christian, obedience is not about a regulated response to a command, but about a life lived in fidelity to the demands of the Gospel. For an illustration of such fidelity we need look no further than Newman himself, not the relatively young man at the height of his influence in Oxford, who is preaching these sermons, but the man he had become more than thirty years later, not yet a

cardinal, who could survey a life shredded by disappointments. It is
the story with which we have become familiar.

He had had his hopes for the Church of England overturned
and his reception into the Catholic Church had brought about a
sorrowful parting from many of his dearest friends. He had
responded generously to various invitations, but had then been let
down: his efforts to found the University in Dublin had been
constantly thwarted; his plans to translate the Bible were allowed
to evaporate; his attempt to support *The Rambler* by taking over as
editor was undermined; his hopes for an Oratory in Oxford were
systematically frustrated. It comes as no surprise to find an entry in
his Journal in 1863, when he had been brought so low, where he
gave vent to his feelings:

> O how forlorn and dreary has been my course since I have
> been a Catholic! ... since I made the great sacrifice, to which
> God called me, He has rewarded me in ten thousand ways, O
> how many! but He has marked my course with unin-
> termittent mortification ... since I have been a Catholic, I
> seem to myself to have had nothing but failure, personally.
> (*A.W.* pp. 254–5)

He was all too familiar with disappointment and a sense of being
defeated. His spirits may have been lowered; nevertheless, as the
gratitude expressed in his Journal showed, he remained faithful.
There is more to be said.

(v)

Central to Newman's understanding of Christian discipleship was his
refusal to concentrate on any one virtue or quality exclusively. The
sermon on saving knowledge was careful to avoid the pitfall which
assumed that a single good quality could be the guarantee of true
holiness. General obedience, many qualities together, make up the
whole. On 25 February 1838, as you listened, you would have heard
Newman speaking about the relationship between faith and love.

There is a sense, he suggested, in which love is 'all virtues at once'. It is the material 'out of which all graces are made'. He described it as a quality of mind, a disposition, in other words, which is the fruit of new life in Christ. Those who are new-born in Christ are rooted in love. And the Spirit dwells in that love. 'Faith and hope are graces of an imperfect state, and they cease with that state; but love is greater, because it is perfection' (*P.S.* iv, p. 309). Love is 'the seed of holiness, and grows into all excellences, not indeed destroying their peculiarities, but making them what they are' (*P.S.* iv, p. 311). 'Faith is the first element of *religion*, and love, of *holiness*; and as holiness and religion are distinct, yet united, so are love and faith' (*P.S.* iv, p. 312). 'Moreover, it is plain', he went on,

> that, while love is the root out of which faith grows, faith by receiving the wonderful tidings of the Gospel, and presenting before the soul its sacred Objects, the mysteries of faith, the Holy Trinity, and the Incarnate Saviour, expands our love, and raises it to a perfection which otherwise it could never reach. And thus our duty lies in faith working by love; . . . . (*P.S.* iv, p. 314–15)

There is much more packed into this sermon which handles so delicately this life-giving relationship, but let us break off at this phrase, 'faith working by love', in effect, '*fides charitate formata*'.

Let us suppose that your enthusiasm for Mr Newman is such that not only do you attend his weekly sermons in St Mary's; the previous year, 1837, you had also gone to listen to his *Lectures on Justification*, delivered in the Adam de Brome Chapel in the University Church. That phrase, faith working by love, might well have stirred in your memory one of those Lectures' most captivating passages. Newman had declared:

> I would treat of faith as it is actually found in the soul; and I say it is as little an isolated grace, as a man is a picture. It has a depth, a breadth, and a thickness; it has an inward life which is something over and above itself; it has a heart, and blood,

and pulses, and nerves, though not upon the surface. All
these indeed are not *spoken* of, when we make mention of
faith; nor are they painted on the canvas; but they are implied
in the word, because they exist in the thing ... Love and
fear, and heavenly-mindedness, and obedience and firmness,
and zeal, and humility, are as certainly one with justifying
faith, considered as a thing existing, as bones, muscles, and
vital organs, are necessary to that outward frame of man
which meets the eye, though they do not meet it. Love and
fear and obedience are not really posterior to justifying faith
for even a moment of time, unless bones and muscles are
formed after the countenance and complexion. It is as
unmeaning to speak of living faith, as being independent of
newness of mind, as of solidity as divisible from body, or
tallness from stature, or colour from landscape. As well might
it be said that an arm or a foot can exist out of the body, and
that man is born with only certain portions, head or heart,
and the rest accrues afterwards, as that faith comes first and
gives birth to other graces (*Jfc.* pp. 265–6).

The virtues weave together to form a seamless web of holiness.

(vi)

If we now ask how Newman viewed the condition of a person in
whom these qualities and virtues had come together, we can turn
to the beginning of his sermon, 'The State of Salvation'. He
preached it on 18 March 1838, which was only six days after he
had finished preparing his *Lectures on Justification* for publication.
He contrasted someone enslaved to sin and filled with darkness to
a person in whom the blessings of Christ have found their home.
'As that which is created differs from what is not created,' he
observed, 'so the Christian differs from the natural man ... As far
as a being can be changed without losing his identity, as far as it is
sense to say that an existing being can be new created, so far has
man this gift when the grace of the Gospel has its perfect work and

its maturity of fruit in him' (*P.S.* v, pp. 178–9). No greater contrast could be imagined. New life in Christ, living faith, brings about what has been called a share in the divine nature. In a Christmas sermon Newman set out this teaching plainly: 'Men we remain, but not mere men, but gifted with a measure of all those perfections which Christ has in fullness, partaking each in his own degree of His Divine Nature so fully, that the only reason (so to speak) why His saints are not really like Him, is that it is impossible – that He is the Creator, and they His creatures; . . .' (*P.S.* viii, p. 253). This is the doctrine of divinisation, proclaimed in Scripture (see 2 Pet. 1:4) and expounded by the Fathers of the Church (see *Ath.* ii, pp. 88–90).

All the same, it would be a mistake to presume that this privileged condition was a panacea. For Newman the contrary was closer to the truth. A fortnight after he had described the state of salvation in such exalted terms, he preached a sermon which is among his most moving. It displays notable psychological perceptiveness. It was called 'Sins of Infirmity'.

On this occasion Newman indicated that the results of faith 'are righteous and holy', but he also acknowledged that 'the process through which they are obtained is one of imperfection'. From a distance, he remarked, the soul of the righteous appears 'youthful in countenance, and bright in apparel; but approach him, and his face has lines of care upon it, and his dress is tattered'. His righteousness has been 'wrought out of sin, the result of a continual struggle, – not spontaneous nature, but habitual self-command'. And he went on: 'True faith is not shown here below in peace, but rather in conflict; . . As we gain happiness through suffering, so do we arrive at holiness through infirmity, because man's very condition is a fallen one, and in passing out of the country of sin, he necessarily passes through it' (*P.S.* v, p. 210). Those who 'venture much with their talents,' he added a little later, 'gain much . . . [but they] cannot believe that they are making any progress; and though they do, yet surely they have much to be forgiven in all their services. They are like David, men of blood; they fight the good fight of faith, but they are polluted with the contest' (*P.S.* v, p. 214).

These few sentences can convey only slightly the effect of the whole; still they may be enough to show that Newman did not regard believing as offering immunity from conflict. Indeed, in 1836, you would have heard him urging you to seek out conflict, when he told you that, as faith is the essence of a Christian life, so there is a duty 'in risking upon Christ's word what we have, for what we have not' (*P.S.* iv, p. 299). We need to make what he called 'ventures of faith', and what I, in part through learning from him, have described elsewhere as 'the risk of discipleship'. We must be prepared to make a commitment and accept the consequences whatever they may be, consequences which are not of our choosing. What virtue is there in living in such a way that it would make no difference to us if Christ's word proved to be false?

(vii)

This chapter may have been more demanding, more difficult than the others, but the earlier chapters will, I hope, have prepared the way for it. I have tried to offer something substantial for reflection by presenting this account of Newman's teaching on faith as it appeared in his pastoral sermons. And we have caught glimpses of his spirituality as well.

At the start it was important to appreciate the circumstances of those times which influenced what he had to say, evangelicalism and liberalism, while it was also necessary to be aware of the convictions which guided him as a preacher, especially his devotion to religion as revealed. We have found him attentive to human experience so that his words would be real, his sermons come alive. We have seen the emphasis he placed on faith as common to everyone, not something peculiar to the religious, and on the part played by witness, testimony. We have also considered the role of conscience as the authority within us, pointing us beyond ourselves. And we have heard his account of the bond between faith and obedience, and not only obedience, but the other virtues as well which are woven together, a seamless robe, an entire disposition which establishes us in a privileged condition before God, which gives us indeed a share in the divine nature, and which bestows on us perfection at the last, but which at first is experienced as conflict. We must be prepared to take risks for Christ's sake. There should be much in this teaching that can speak to us still.

Earlier, I compared your memories to Matthew Arnold's. Let us return to him once more.

What Arnold had said he had seemed to hear was a passage from a sermon called 'Peace in Believing'. Newman preached it first in May 1839. He offered comfort, the reward of a living faith: 'After the fever of life; after wearinesses and sicknesses; fightings and despondings; languor and fretfulness; struggling and failing, struggling and succeeding; after all the changes and chances of this troubled unhealthy state, at length comes death, at length the White Throne of God, at length the Beatific Vision' (*P.S.* vi, pp. 369–70). Now, it has been suggested that Arnold in fact would have heard Newman only rarely, but that matters little to us. Rather the contrary. For, if it is true, the vividness of his memory reveals the power of the impression which the preacher made on him. And we know that such impressions are not commonly composed out of theory. Arnold's clear memory bears witness to the reality of Newman's experience.

10

Witness to Holiness

(i)

For twelve years it was my good fortune to be one of the Catholic chaplains at Oxford University. During that time, whenever I said Mass in the Chaplaincy, I celebrated it in a chapel dedicated to St Thomas More. There was, however, one exception. At 11 o'clock on Sundays, especially during term, that chapel could not accommodate the numbers that came, and so Mass was celebrated in the large hall. It was called the Newman Room. For those years, therefore, that central act of my ministry as Catholic chaplain was celebrated in a place associated either with More or Newman, two Englishmen acclaimed by many for their holiness. My particular concern here, of course, is with Newman, but, in considering his witness to holiness it will be helpful to keep an eye on Thomas More as well, noticing what he and Newman had in common as well as where there were contrasts.

More, for example, has been described as born for friendship, yet we know that he loved solitude and retained throughout his life a sympathy for the Carthusian vocation which he had tried as a young man. And Newman, as we have seen, wrote in 1829 of the 'Blessings of friends, which to my door, unask'd, unhoped, have come' (*V.V.* p. 46), yet he was also said to be never less alone than when alone. In 1868 he even commented: 'I have often been puzzled at myself, that I should be both particularly fond of being alone, and particularly fond of being with friends' (*L.D.* xxiv, p. 53). It is relevant as well to remember the influence of the Charterhouse on the Oratorian way of life.

Then there is the irony of the contrast between their public and private faces. More is fixed in the popular imagination as a man of wit, satire, and good humour, a merry man; people tend to forget the darker, more pessimistic side. Newman, on the other hand, is generally thought of as humourless, austere and forbidding; however, as we have noticed before, he could be funny, and often too in ways reminiscent of More, dry wit, satirical perception, and a deadpan humour which could leave people unsure whether there was a joke or not.[1] I think, for instance, of the reservation he expressed in a letter in 1877 about an Anglican sermon of his because it contained the phrase, 'the Church has erred'. The phrase, he said, grated on him. Then he added, 'I should not mind "the Pope has erred"' (*L.D.* xxviii, p. 274). Again, Thomas More was devoted to education. Public life may have limited his contribution to humanist studies, but his place in the new learning is assured. And Newman, as we have seen time and again, was devoted to education; it was 'his line', one of the major concerns that governed his life. And then there was conscience which Newman famously would toast before toasting the Pope (see *Diff.* ii, p. 261), and to which More adhered, maintaining thereby his communion with the Pope, although himself in fact no extreme papalist, and thereby losing his life.

Friendship and solitude, humour and gravity, education and conscience, these are some of the threads which bind these two men to each other. But my main concern is with holiness and here their paths may seem to diverge, one a martyr, the other dying peacefully in his bed. But before we consider the contrast, we should remember what holiness entails.

(ii)

Christian holiness must never be diminished to an abstraction. We must look steadily at Jesus of Nazareth, that man, his life, and learn from him. We call him saviour and in the past it has been common to locate his saving work in his crucifixion: Jesus saved us by dying on the cross. More recently, however, the part played in our

---

1 See above, pp. 5–6.

redemption by the resurrection has been restored. And more than that, we must acknowledge the significance of the birth of the Christ as well, and his hidden life, and his public ministry. In other words, the significance of Jesus of Nazareth can never be reduced to the events of a particular Friday afternoon. His birth, his hidden life and public ministry, his death on the cross and resurrection to glory are all of a piece. The entire sequence of events is salvific, because it gives expression to something else, something interior, something within.

Jesus of Nazareth was the faithful one. His whole existence was shaped by an interior disposition of perfect love and obedience. He loved his heavenly Father and was obedient to his will; he loved all men and women and was obedient to, at the service of, their need: because of sin, they needed to be saved. It was the Father's will that he minister to that need. There was a perfect correspondence in his obedience. Jesus was faithful.

To place such emphasis on interior disposition should not lead us to neglect the external events. The human condition is a unity composed of both. There is a fine interweaving. Interior reality has external consequences. It is vital to realise that our salvation was achieved not because Jesus mindlessly followed a pre-arranged programme of events that led to his crucifixion, but because he was utterly faithful to the Father's will and our needs and so he accepted the consequences of that fidelity, however terrible they might be. So when the Gospel speaks of holiness and urges us to be Christ-like, it is not imposing on us trials and sufferings, arbitrarily conceived, but encouraging us to develop an interior life which equips us for the testing that will follow. Testing is the inevitable consequence of this kind of fidelity, fashioned within, in a sin-scarred world.

The life and death of Jesus were of a piece. But at once we realise there is a distinction that has to be made. He, the Word made flesh, may have given us an example of perfect fidelity, but that cannot be expected of us. We know all too well that our lives do not display that consistency. There is always a need for growth and there will be a crisis. Given that each one's pilgrimage is unique, these two elements – of growth and of crisis – seem to be the most common. And here More and Newman offer a striking contrast.

(iii)

Thomas More obviously had a crisis, he was martyred; but where, it might be asked, was the growth? Was he not, in Erasmus's famous phrase, the title of Robert Bolt's play, 'a man for all seasons', outstandingly well-rounded and well-integrated? But if those words are understood as abstracting him from his own season, then they do not do him justice. He cannot be removed from his own time and place. Nobody can. He was not so much a man for all seasons as a man for every season, because he was a man of his own season, deeply involved in the issues and demands of his day. We should admire him not because he somehow held himself aloof from them, but because, while he struggled with them, he was not absorbed by them. He was not at their mercy. He felt the call of solitude, but longed also to be married; he wrestled with his desire for scholarship, but was drawn to the demands of his professional life; he studied and understood the truth about the nature of the Church, although throughout his life its appearance was largely unlovely; and he recognised the implications of the king's great matter, his divorce, and stood firm to resist them.

I am not suggesting that Thomas More swept along some high road of supreme virtue, untouched by compromise, misgiving or failure. Nobody does that. The famous wit could wound as well as make merry; the polemical pamphlets, salted with scatology and relentless invective, hardly accord with an image of saintliness; he was ambitious; and he persecuted heretics with zeal. He would have understood without difficulty Newman's remark that 'True faith is not shown here below in peace, but rather in conflict', and that 'in passing out of the country of sin, [man] necessarily passes through it' (*P.S.* v, p. 210). More limped along often enough. If he can be honoured as a saint, however, it is not merely because he was martyred or by turning a blind eye to his failings. We are not required to like the language of the pamphlets or applaud the persecution of heretics. Thomas More is a saint because he grew in holiness. He had struggled with the choices placed before him. Then, when his time came to die, he was prepared. His death was of a piece with what had gone before. He had worked to fashion his fidelity from the complexities and ambiguities of his own experience.

What, however, are we to say about Newman?

(iv)

If Thomas More is remembered especially for the crisis of his martyrdom, Newman is remembered especially for development, not only of doctrinal theory, but of the personal journey. Let me recall briefly the main moments which by now are familiar enough.

Born in 1801 and brought up in an Anglican home with a thorough knowledge of the Bible, he underwent a kind of evangelical conversion when he was fifteen. Its effects lingered for some years, but as a young fellow of Oriel in 1822, in a common room which was said to stink of logic, he came under the influence of Richard Whately, sturdy logician, eccentric character, and future Anglican Archbishop of Dublin. He drew Newman out of his shy shell and through Whately Newman was touched by Oriel's rationalism. But soon he was affected still more by other friends, notably Hurrell Froude, Edward Pusey, and John Keble. Their friendship, his own illness in 1827, and the death of his sister, Mary, in 1828, brought him to recognise the limitations of intellectual excellence alone. Then in 1833, responding to what he and his friends saw as a crisis within the Church of England, he preached and lectured and campaigned with them to arouse in his fellow Anglicans a keener sense of their own heritage within the Catholic tradition. By 1841, however, the understanding of the Anglican Church which he had advocated seemed to him to have been repudiated. He was on his death-bed in the Church of England from that time. On 9 October 1845, after immense heart-searching, he was received into the Roman Catholic Church. Newman had moved from evangelicalism through rationalism into a perception of the Church of England as Catholic and then on from there to Roman Catholicism. He had been growing; he had been on pilgrimage.

At the same time, it is important to realise that this movement was not evidence of restlessness for its own sake, but a consequence of his tireless search for the fullness of Christian truth. As a Catholic too he probed the great mysteries of faith and anyone who knows Newman well will acknowledge the truth of his remark to an evangelical correspondent, George Edwards, to whom he wrote in 1887. He was eighty-six at the time. He spoke of 'those great and burning truths, which I learned when a boy from evangelical teaching', and which he had 'found impressed upon my heart with fresh and ever increasing force by the Holy Roman Church' (*L.D.* xxxi, p. 189). Newman's thought developed, but remained also remarkably consistent. He was a pilgrim, not a religious wanderlust. But was he a saint?

'By their fruits you shall know them.' It is a wise test of sanctity. The fruits of Newman's work have been considerable. His writings have touched vast numbers of people. Many of his sermons have a power still which time has not dimmed. His influence on religious thought has been wide-ranging. His *Essay on the Development of Christian Doctrine* in 1845, imperfect and, indeed, unfinished as it was, opened up an area vital for the Church's self-understanding. Since the Second Vatican Council a stream of books and articles has appeared, arguing that Newman had anticipated ideas which the Council had emphasised, for example, on the papacy, the laity, and on ecumenism, and there are deeper currents as well.[2] The fruits of his work have been extensive. All

---

2 The situation, of course, has moved on since the Second Vatican Council ended in 1965. To explore the matter further, compare B. C. Butler, 'Newman and the Second Vatican Council', in Coulson and Allchin (eds.), *The Rediscovery of Newman*, pp. 233–46; and Nicholas Lash, 'Tides and Twilight: Newman since Vatican II', in Ker and Hill (eds.), *Newman after a Hundred Years*, pp. 447–64.

the same, people are not canonised simply for their writing. When Newman himself is considered as a man, two main criticisms tend to be expressed.

(v)

First of all, he is thought to have been too sensitive. In his dealings with people he seems to have been extremely touchy. The suggestion has often been made that whether it was Oxford colleagues, fellow Oratorians, or Church authorities, he took offence far too easily and could be waspish in reply. Various comments can be made. On the one hand, I suspect that Newman's own clarity of thought made him a rigorous critic of even passing remarks, which at times lent those remarks a weight they were never intended to carry. He may not always have been the most comfortable person to live with. Then, on the other hand, the charge of excessive sensitivity, offered as a bar to sanctity, falls into the trap of implying that only people with certain temperaments can truly be holy. Obviously that will not do. There are no privileged or handicapped temperaments. Holiness is available to all: it depends on the way we handle the raw material.

The second criticism is more serious. In effect it argues that when Charles Kingsley wrote, 'Truth, for its own sake, is not a virtue with the Roman clergy. Father Newman informs us that it need not, and on the whole ought not to be', he was in a way right. Most obviously, of course, he was wrong, but the suspicion lingers that he had pointed to a real weakness. If that suspicion has any basis, then I suggest it has to do with a problem common among intellectual people. Those who are skilful at marshalling arguments may well be in danger of being able to present a case so effectively that a false position may pass as true. It is almost an occupational hazard for the intellectual.

For the sake of argument, therefore, let us suppose that Newman was as hypersensitive as people have sometimes suggested, and let us suppose that his very gifts of mind made him a prey to the hazards of advocacy. We can then learn two lessons about holiness.

First, that if a person is a saint, that does not mean they have always been so. As Newman himself observed, even among the greatest saints, there are those who 'in early life were committed to very un-saintly doings' (*H.S.* ii, p. 341). It is the point with which this book began, the point echoed by Pope Benedict XVI, when he observed, 'Holiness does not consist in never having erred or sinned.'[3] The discovery of some failing, even serious, is no necessary disqualification from holiness. Newman, like Thomas More, had failings which he had to struggle to overcome.

More seriously, however, this attitude which would regard a person who has sinned as incapable of holiness is dangerously mistaken. There is a danger because, although sinning is not essential to being human, it is in fact inescapable (without the privilege granted to the Mother of Jesus, but that is another question). It follows that to identify holiness with sinlessness is either to make it altogether unattainable or to remove it from the realm of ordinary human life. It is ironical that the very people who say, 'Thomas More isn't a saint; he persecuted heretics', or 'Newman cannot be canonised; he was shifty', are the same people who would be most opposed to that uncritical attitude to the saints which we call hagiography, while their standpoint implies that, if holiness ever were achieved, it could only be of a kind which would invite that extreme hagiography which they most deplore. We need to be clear. We can become holy, even though we have sinned and maybe sinned grievously. We do so, not by suppressing our humanity, but by bringing it, after much struggling, whole and entire, into a harmonious relationship with the Spirit of Christ which dwells within us. We grow into holiness and accept the consequences.

It is clear then that Newman was a pilgrim. He grew in holiness. But he died in old age, a Cardinal of the Roman Church, held in high esteem by his countrymen. Where, it might be asked, was the crisis? Was there a crisis? The Gospels tell us that there has to be, because 'whoever does not bear the cross and follow me, cannot

---

3 See above, p. ix.

be my disciple' (Luke 16:27). How many of us hear those words and wonder about them? What cross do we bear, you and I? In Thomas More's case, the cross is evident. He was martyred. But what about us? What about Newman?

(vi)

Years ago, when I was first ordained and people came to see me in distress, because of illness, or because a husband or wife had died, or because their career plans had been disappointed and their gifts frustrated, I used to see them as exceptions. That was partly because I was young and partly because I had been fortunate. Experience soon taught me otherwise. Virtually everyone has to face crisis, often more than one. Crises are like defeats. They have no relieving features. It is never good to be handicapped, for a loved one to die, for people to be unemployed, for gifts to be squandered. It may be, in fact, that those who are handicapped accept the challenge of their disability and give an outstanding example of courage, that the bereaved person remarries happily in due course, that talents acquired are not wasted in the end, but the sense of defeat at the time is none the less devastating. It is a crucifixion. These people are as defeated in these ways as Jesus was on Calvary. We must not take advantage of the hindsight Easter supplies. Jesus had been perfectly faithful to his Father's will; he had spent himself in love for everyone; yet his love was rejected and his ministry lay in ruins. The essence of crucifixion is not wood and nails, but defeat.

Newman's life offers us many examples. We have become familiar with them. His hopes for the Church of England were rejected and his reception into the Catholic Church brought about a terrible parting from many of his closest friends: Keble's letter, asking for forgiveness for a seventeen-year silence, is particularly moving (see *L.D.* xx, pp. 501–2). And then there were those enterprises of his Catholic years, the founding of the University in Dublin, his translation of the Bible, the invitation to edit *The Rambler*, and his hopes for an Oratory in Oxford; his plans and efforts seemed always to be undermined and frustrated. And there were the clashes as well with people like Manning and Faber and W. G. Ward. He knew himself to be an object of pity and contempt. By the early 1860s his days were dark and it comes as no surprise to read that entry in his Journal in 1863 which we have noted before. It is instructive to see it again in this context:

> O how forlorn and dreary has been my course since I have been a Catholic! . . . since I made the great sacrifice, to which God called me, He has rewarded me in ten thousand ways, O how many! but he has marked my course with almost unintermittent mortification . . . since I have been a Catholic, I seem to myself to have had nothing but failure, personally. (*A.W.* pp. 254-5)

Newman knew intimately that defeat which lies at the heart of crucifixion, and his dark hours can alert us to recognise when we too are being tested. Everyone goes through such a crisis. And if it arouses intense self-pity, then the defeat can smother us and will indeed be death-dealing. But if a person can somehow remain generous, open-hearted, loving, even at such a time, then it is possible to move on from disaster to new life.[4] In these times of crisis, when defeat seems heaviest, fidelity is the key. As Jesus even on Calvary commended himself into his Father's hands, so was he raised from the dead. We find that same vital steadfastness in those who seek holiness.

Thomas More's son-in-law, William Roper, has recorded for us More's remark at their parting, 'Son Roper, I thank our Lord, the field is won', words that Roper understood to mean that 'it was for the love he had to God wrought in him so effectually, that it conquered in him all his carnal affections utterly'.[5] And we may remember how Newman, after suffering and withstanding so many disappointments, particularly as a Catholic, learnt finally that he was to be made a Cardinal. That, of course, was only a human

---

4 See Strange, *The Catholic Faith*, pp. 29–31.
5 William Roper, *Life of More*, (London, 1938), p. 50.

judgement, but it lifted from his name and from his writings the insidious, damaging suspicion that his views were unreliable, unsound. As he told his old friend, Mother Mary Imelda Poole: 'It is a wonderful Providence, that even before my death that acquittal of me comes, which I knew would come some day or other, though not in my life time' (*L.D.* xxix, p. 63). He had been proved wrong.

(vii)

The way Thomas More died is well known. He was beheaded on the scaffold. His composure, his grace, his good humour did not desert him, as he waited for the axe to fall. He died 'in and for the faith of the Holy Catholic Church'.[6] He died a martyr. The manner of Newman's death is less well known. The final days were described by Father William Neville, Newman's secretary and carer in his later years.

On 9 August 1890, he has said, Newman came into his room and his step was at first unrecognised, it seemed so firm and elastic; and he was 'unbent, erect to the full height of his years in the fifties'. His carriage was 'soldier-like, and so dignified; and his countenance was most attractive to look at; even great age', Neville remarked, 'seemed to have gone from his face, and with it all careworn signs; his very look conveyed the cheerfulness and gratitude of his mind, and what he said was so kind; his voice was quite fresh and strong, his whole appearance was that of power, combined with complete calm . . .'[7] However, he became ill that night with congestion. He got up the next morning, but he had to return to bed later and the following day, 11 August, at about a quarter to nine in the evening, he died. He had been unconscious for most of the day.

The gentleness of his passing makes a vivid contrast with the violence of More's. Yet both of them had striven for fidelity. One

---

6 Roper, *Life of More*, p. 70.
7 See Wilfrid Ward, *The Life of Cardinal Newman* ii, p. 537.

died on the scaffold, the other in bed, but both had nourished their interior lives to grow in holiness and been confronted by external crisis. By remaining faithful they had turned defeat into victory, passing from death to new life. As a younger man, Newman had already expressed the matter most simply: 'The planting of Christ's Cross in the heart is sharp and trying; but the stately tree rears itself aloft, and has fair branches and rich fruit, and is good to look upon' (*P.S.* iv, p. 262).

11

The Flame of Love

(i)

When the news broke that Newman had died, tributes poured in which bore witness to the esteem in which he was widely held throughout the country. As we have seen, it had not always been like that. Forty-five years earlier, when he had left the Church of England and become a Roman Catholic, many of those whom he left looked upon him with contempt, while those whom he had joined, the small Catholic community, lacking in self-confidence, were unsure how to use his gifts and regarded him with suspicion.

This combination of contempt and suspicion gradually led to forgetfulness and neglect until, nineteen years later, Charles Kingsley casually accused him of indifference to the truth. The injustice of that charge in particular Newman found insupportable and, as we know, it provoked the correspondence which caused him to write his *Apologia pro Vita Sua* in which he described the steps that had led to his conversion to Catholicism. He was vindicated triumphantly, as old friends acknowledged the honesty of his actions and, moreover, were surprised and moved to discover the continuing warmth of his affection for them, while new friends began to recognise the calibre of his gifts. As we have realised, it was one of the great turning-points in his life. It restored to him the respect of many which had been lacking for so long.

Thus restored, early the following year, in January 1865, he felt compelled to write again. The subject was very different. He has described his mood: 'On the 17th of January it came into my head to write it. I really cannot tell you how, and I wrote on till it was finished, on small bits of paper. And I could no more write anything else by willing it, than I could fly' (*L.D.* xxii, p. 72). What he was writing in this way was his long poem, *The Dream of Gerontius*. It seems fitting to draw these reflections on Newman to a close by exploring some aspects of this poem about death and judgement. It is a kind of coda.

(ii)

The Dream of Gerontius tells of the death of a man of faith who has lived life to the full. He is a good man, but not a saint. To put it simply, Gerontius has been saved; he will go to heaven; but first he must be purified. There is a purgatory for him to undergo. In Newman's poem, we accompany him from his death-bed to his judgement.

After its publication in *The Month*, later the same year, it attracted praise from many quarters. Thomas Brown, the Catholic bishop of Newport, was one who wrote to Newman to express his admiration. Six years earlier he had been the cause of Newman coming under suspicion in Rome by reporting him to the authorities there for his views on the place of the laity in the Church. Newman, in acknowledging Brown's letter, observed, 'It is a great gratification to me to receive your Lordship's approbation on any thing which I have written' (*L.D.* xxii, p. 39). We may imagine that he was smiling as he chose his words. Then Gladstone, who was soon to become Prime Minister for the first time, wrote in 1868, when *The Dream* appeared in a volume of Newman's poems. He told him that he had read *Gerontius* several times and he compared it to Dante's *Divina Commedia* (*L.D.* xxiv, p. 7, n.1). And soon afterwards Newman's old Oriel friend, Richard Church, made the same comparison in a review. Newman replied that such praise made him blush and passed it off with a comic reference. 'Do you remember the story of bashful and humble Tom Churton?' he asked Church; 'how at some great Ashmolean gathering he gently breathed into something that looked like a wind instrument – and what followed?' (*L.D.* xxiv, p. 42) Church did not; he could only guess.

The poem grew in popularity. Newman heard of a farmer 'who

took to it, when he was ill – it was to him a prayer or meditation' (*L.D.* xxv, p. 209). And much later he was moved to learn that General Gordon had used it while in Egypt and had had it with him in Khartoum. Gordon had then given it to *The Times* correspondent, Frank Power, who was later killed. Power's sister lent Newman the copy for a while (see *L.D.* xxxi, pp. 51–2). 'What struck me so much in his [Gordon's] use of "The Dream etc.,"' he told another friend, Frederic Rogers, Lord Blachford, 'was that in St Paul's words he "died daily" – he was always on his death bed, fulfilling the common advice that we should ever pass the day, as if it was to be our last' (*L.D.* xxxi, p. 67).

Gordon had come to know about the poem during a long conversation with a friend about death. He had been telling him how his spiritual life had changed when he gazed on his father's lifeless body and found himself thinking, 'Is this what we all come to?' His friend told him that some of his ideas reminded him of Newman's *Dream of Gerontius*. Gordon then asked for a copy and had one sent on to him. He received it in Egypt and must have read it on the way to the Sudan, marking the text in pencil. These were the markings which took Newman's breath away when he saw them (see *L.D.* xxxi, pp. 51–2).

'Is that what we all come to?' Gordon's question is common, whether asked of others or kept to ourselves. After my ordination as a priest, I was surprised how often people asked me about life after death. It was as though my new state was assumed to give me fresh light on the subject. We find it absorbing. Newman's poem has regularly helped people to understand it, but it does not tell the whole story or even pretend to. Newman made the point plainly himself. A priest wrote to him almost at once on the poem's publication, full of praise, but regretting the slight mention made of the Blessed Virgin. Newman answered him: ' . . . you do me too much honour, if you think I am to see in a dream everything that *has* to be seen in the *subject* dreamed about . . . It is not my fault if the sleeper did not dream more. Perhaps something woke him. Dreams are generally fragmentary. I have nothing more to tell' (*L.D.* xxi, p. 498).

We may be aware of other limitations: in particular, the poem is intensely individualistic and neglects almost completely any reference to the final judgement of the entire human race. Yet it is only a dream, fragmentary, partial; we should not ask of it answers it was never intended to supply. In fact, I suspect that it is so popular because it speaks to our real, personal concerns. Theologians may speculate on the great Last Judgement; most of us are more preoccupied with our own. And in *The Dream* we find that three of our most deeply-rooted anxieties are addressed: the fear of perpetual extinction, the fear of judgement, and the fear of what that judgement will entail. To make such a claim for Newman's poem may seem extravagant at first, but often we do not notice what we are hearing at a deeper level. We have to heighten our awareness. Let me set the scene.

(iii)

Gerontius, we know, is not supposed to be a candidate for canonisation. Although a believer, he is a man of the world, who has committed his share of sins and needs to be forgiven. The opening section of the poem which takes us to the moment of his death gives us a portrait of the man. First of all, he is a realist. He recognises that his end is near; no room is left for self-deception: 'Jesu, Maria – ' he exclaims, 'I am near to death, and Thou art calling me; I know it now' (*V.V.* p. 323). And he calls on his friends to pray for him: 'So pray for me, my friends, who have not strength to pray' (*V.V.* p. 324).

This need for their prayers is sharpened by his own fear. What does he fear? General Gordon's question, 'Is this what we all come to?' expresses it exactly. The terror that grips him is the threat of perpetual extinction, of his annihilation. He speaks of his very being giving way, 'As though I was no more a substance now', of his decay as unavoidable, so that he must 'drop from out the universal frame / Into that shapeless, scopeless, blank abyss, / That utter nothingness, of which I came' (*V.V.* p. 324). His words capture the horror many feel when death approaches.

But Gerontius is not a coward. He rallies bravely: 'Rouse thee, my fainting soul, and play the man; ... Prepare to meet thy God ... Use well the interval' (*V.V.* p. 325). Nor is this courage bravado. While his friends pray for him, his own appeal to God for mercy soars into a stirring act of faith in the Trinity and the Incarnation of the Son:

> Firmly I believe and truly
>> God is Three, and God is One;
> And I next acknowledge duly
>> Manhood taken by the Son.

He proclaims his trust and hope in the redemption won by the cross of Christ, affirms his veneration for the Church and her teachings, accepts with the joy the severance of earthly ties, and concludes in adoration 'To the God of earth and heaven, / Father, Son, and Holy Ghost' (*V.V.* pp. 327–8). Then the sense of horror returns and now with resignation he appeals to Jesus, Mary and Joseph, and commends himself to God: 'Into Thy hands, / O Lord, into Thy hands ...' (*V.V.* p. 330). And he dies. But the question remains: is there anything more? Is this what we all come to?

(iv)

Newman at once begins to supply the answer. It is not just that Gerontius has survived death; it is the character of his new condition. If the root of our fear of death is the fear of annihilation, then that dread is for Gerontius laid altogether to rest, for, having died, he discovers, not nothingness, but a degree of self-possession, of self-awareness, that overwhelms him:

> I went to sleep; and now I am refresh'd,
> A strange refreshment: for I feel in me
> An inexpressive lightness, and a sense
> Of freedom, as I were at length myself,
> And ne'er had been before. (*V.V.* pp. 331–2).

Here is a suggestion of that full knowledge, that full understanding, that comes from being fully understood (see 1 Cor. 13:12). And this wholeness shows itself in various ways. His self-knowledge puts everything into perspective:

> ... now I am
> So whole of heart, so calm, so self-possess'd,
> With such a full content, and with a sense
> So apprehensive and discriminant,
> As no temptation can intoxicate. (*V.V.* p. 338)

Even judgement holds no fears for him:

> Now that the hour is come, my fear is fled;
> And at this balance of my destiny,
> Now close upon me, I can look forward
> With a serenest joy. (*V.V.* p. 341).

So the fear of perpetual extinction is dispatched by the presentation of the clear alternative: instead of annihilation we come to know ourselves with a completeness and a perfection never attained before. And this self-knowledge is crucial, for it contains the key to the conquest of the other fears as well, the fear of judgement and the punishment which follows. These fears form an alliance. They make themselves more terrible by creating a dilemma: either annihilation or, if not, an unknown judgment and unspeakable punishment. That is a common, popular perception of our destiny. But if, when we die, we find ourselves revealed completely to ourselves, we discover by that very token that our judgement is not arbitrary. We are not going to be judged, as we may have feared, according to some surprise, unseen syllabus. Our own earthly lives will be the subject of judgement and our self-knowledge can foresee the verdict. Gerontius looks forward to it with 'a serenest joy'. A hymn for those who have died, which Newman had composed eight years earlier, had anticipated the same idea:

> For daily falls, for pardon'd crime,
>   They joy to undergo
> The shadow of Thy cross sublime,
>   The remnant of Thy woe. (*V.V.* p. 315).

Judgement will not be alien. Our perfect self-knowledge will invite it, welcome it. We will delight in being purified of every imperfection. But does that resolve the third fear, of what that purification might involve? Even with our present, imperfect self-knowledge we recognise that we have done wrong, that we have sinned. We must face the consequences and Catholic tradition speaks of our purification as purgatorial fire. Won't that fire be terrible, fearsome? But in the fire we find the answer to our fear.

We may associate fire with pain and punishment, but fire is also a symbol of love. When we love most deeply, we may say we are afire with love. As his Guardian Angel warns Gerontius by reminding him of the stigmata experienced by St Francis of Assisi, to come into the presence of this love is to be refined as by fire:

> There was a mortal who is now above
> In the mid glory: he, when near to die,
> Was given communion with the Crucified, –
> Such, that the Master's very wounds were stamp'd
> Upon his flesh; and, from the agony
> Which thrill'd through body and soul in that embrace,
> Learn that the flame of the Everlasting Love
> Doth burn ere it transform ... (*V.V.* p. 352)

And so Gerontius is brought to judgement, to the punishment which he must undergo. In what does it consist? In torture? In gratuitous pain? No. He is judged by the sight of his redeemer and his purification flows from that. As the Angel explains:

> It is the face of the Incarnate God
> Shall smite thee with that keen and subtle pain;
>   ...
> The sight of Him will kindle in thy heart

All tender, gracious, reverential thoughts.
Thou wilt be sick with love, and yearn for Him,
And feel as though thou couldst but pity Him,
That one so sweet should e'er have placed Himself
At disadvantage such, as to be used
So vilely by a being so vile as thee.
There is a pleading in His pensive eyes
Will pierce thee to the quick, and trouble thee.
And thou wilt hate and loathe thyself; for, though
Now sinless, thou wilt feel that thou hast sinn'd,
As never thou didst feel; and wilt desire
To slink away, and hide thee from His sight:
And yet wilt have a longing ay to dwell
Within the beauty of His countenance.
And these two pains, so counter and so keen, –
The longing for Him, when thou seest Him not;
The shame of self at thought of seeing Him, –
Will be thy veriest, sharpest purgatory.
(*V.V.* pp. 358, 359–60).

The sight of the Christ will inspire the most profound love and cause both longing for union and shame at wrong-doing. The fire that punishes is welcomed because it is a fire of love that purifies and gives life. It conquers Gerontius utterly.

When he goes before his Judge, he is 'scorch'd and shrivell'd' by the holiness of the Crucified, 'consum'd, yet quicken'd, by the glance of God' (*V.V.* p. 366). His judgement is self-judgement. He is stricken with his unworthiness, overwhelmed by love. He begs to be taken away 'That sooner I may rise, and go above, / And see Him in the truth of everlasting day' (*V.V.* p. 367). In the union with God, the fire of love which in purgatory, the Angel had warned Gerontius, was 'without its light' (*V.V.* p. 351), now gives light, enlightens, brings understanding, the truth of everlasting day.

Among our many fears, these three – of annihilation, judgement, and punishment – wield unnerving power. Newman has mastered them with simplicity. When we die, we do not pass away, nor are we diminished; rather, Newman says, we are at last our true selves. God is love. If we die in his friendship, we are overcome by a love which, like a fire, refines us, transforms us, and draws us into its perfect light.

(v)

A copy of *The Dream of Gerontius* with General Gordon's markings, which Newman was so moved to see, was among the wedding presents given in 1899 to Edward Elgar. He was familiar with the poem already. Some years earlier, in 1892, he had already considered composing an oratorio based on the text and it was perhaps a chance meeting with the lawyer, Edward Bellasis, another of Newman's lifelong friends, that spurred him on to begin the work. It was ready for the Birmingham Festival in 1900 and, although the first performance was generally judged to be a disaster of choral confusion, the piece itself was acclaimed. Since then, of course, it has come to be counted among Elgar's finest work, not least because the music he composed displayed such sympathy with the vision of divine love that Newman's poem reveals.

That vision guided Newman's life.

Index